FOREX TRADING STRATEGIES

THE ULTIMATE BEGINNERS GUIDE ON HOW TO INVEST FOR A LIVING IN THE CURRENCY MARKET USING THE SIMPLE SWING AND DAY TRADE TECHNIQUES (PSYCHOLOGY BASICS EXPLAINED)

Logan Trade

Forex collection Vol 4

© Copyright 2020

© **Copyright 2020 - Logan Trade - All rights reserved.**

The content contained within this book may not be reproduced, duplicated or transmitted without direct written permission from the author or the publisher under no circumstances will any blame or legal responsibility be held against the publisher, or author, for any damages, reparation, or monetary loss due to the information contained within this book. Either directly or indirectly.

Legal Notice:

This book is copyright protected. This book is only for personal use. You cannot amend, distribute, sell, use, quote or paraphrase any part, or the content within this book, without the consent of the author or publisher.

Disclaimer Notice:

Please note the information contained within this document is for educational and entertainment purposes only. All effort has been executed to present accurate, up to date, and reliable, complete information. No warranties of any kind are declared or implied. Readers acknowledge that the author is not engaging in the rendering of legal, financial, medical or professional advice. The content within this book has been derived from various sources. Please consult a licensed professional before attempting any techniques outlined in this book.

By reading this document, the reader agrees that under no circumstances is the author responsible for any losses, direct or indirect, which are incurred as a result of the use of information contained within this document, including, but not limited to, — errors, omissions, or inaccuracies.

Sommario

Forex Advantages 9

Chapter 1. What Is Forex Trading? Overview and history of Forex Trading   15

Forex Trading Terminology 21

Finding the Right Broker Firm 24

Opening the First Trade 26

Chapter 2. Which Currencies are There and Which are the Best Ones to Trade   Us Dollar (Usd) 28

Euro (EUR) 29

Japanese Yen (Jpy) 31

British Pound (Gbp) 32

Swiss Franc (Chf) 32

Australian Dollar (Aud) 33

Canadian Dollar (Cad) 34

Other Currencies 34

Currency Pairs 36

Currency Quotations 37

Chapter 3. Who Can Trade On the Forex Market? 39

IG 40

Saxo Bank 42

CMC Markets 43

City Index 44

XTB Review 45

Choosing Of A Broker And A Trading Platform 45

Chapter 4. Different Existing Trading Styles According to Personal Taste And/Or Available Portfolio 52

Day Trading 53

Swing Trading 54

Scalping Trading 55

Position Trading 56

Forex Trading Strategies 57

Range Trading Strategy 58

Trend Trading Strategy 60

Pairs Trade 61

Price Action Trading 61

Carry Trade Strategy 62

Momentum Trading 63

Pivot Points 65

Fundamental Analysis 65

Forex Strategies For Beginners 66

Forex Breakout Strategy 68

Chapter 5. What Is Fundamental Analysis? 71

Gdp 83

Rate Of Employment 83

Inflation Rate 84

Balance Of Payments 85

Public Debt 86

Interest Rate 86

Chapter 6. Is Technical Analysis Important in Forex Trading? .. 89

History 90

The Benefits Of Technical Analysis In Options Trading 90

Technical Analysis Secrets To Become The Best Trader 95

Importance Of A Technical Analysis 99

Support And Resistance 103

Chapter 7. Resistance and Dynamic Supports 110

Candlesticks 110

Pin Bar Pattern 113

Engulfing Pattern 115

Morning Star / Evening Star 115

Operational Risk Reward 116

Stop Loss And Take Profit 117

Money Management 117

Reversal Signals 118

Drawing Trend Lines 118

Simple Moving Averages 120

Patience Is The Key *122*

Chapter 8. Practical Trading Strategies 124

Analysis-Based Trading Strategies *125*

Trading-Style Based Strategies *129*

Order-Types Trading Strategies *132*

Chapter 9. Winning Psychology for Trading 135

Be Patient... *135*

Be Objective *136*

Be Disciplined *136*

Be Realistic *137*

1 Trust The Process *138*

2 Outline Daily Activities *138*

3 Analyze The Market *139*

4 Be Defensive *139*

5 Have A Trading Plan *140*

6 Know That Trading Is A Business..................................... *140*

7 Outline Risk.. *140*

8 Use Technology...*141*

9 Have A Stop Loss *141*

10 Focus On The Bigger Picture *142*

11 Keep Learning Markets *142*

12 Be A Progressive Trader *142*

Conclusion **144**

Introduction

Forex trading has many favorable aspects, but just like every other trading activity, it has a downside. Every trader that seeks to enter the trade system must assess the advantages and disadvantages of foreign exchange before they make a decision in the appropriateness and attractiveness of the market.

Forex Advantages

Forex exchange has a large number of advantages regardless of the risks; therefore, it makes an attractive and lucrative activity.

The advantages include:

Leverage

Leverage provides traders with substantial opportunities for them to trade and make profits. Access to leverage largely determines the difference between small profits and large ones. In the foreign exchange market, there are more resources for leverage than other markets and depending on the location from which a trader is working from one can get the resource they need. A trader may be able to access a margin that supports leverage of 100:1 or more for the initial capital.

Fast returns

The foreign exchange market moves very fast, and the liquidity is very deep. When the speed, liquidity, and high leverage are combined in the forex market, they create great opportunities for the trader to make exponential profits in the trade more than other markets. In some other markets, the traders have to wait for very long and still get limited returns.

Easy "short selling"

In some other markets, short selling may require a trader to borrow assets and get exposed to risks, but in the forex exchange, short selling currencies have a simpler process. Foreign exchange works in a way that the trader buys one currency while selling the other. In other words, the currencies are traded in pairs. Traders speculate the inclines and declines of different currencies, therefore, sell the losing currency and buy the winning pair without involving a borrowing process.

Liquidity

Because the forex market is the largest market in the world by volume, there are many participants; therefore, liquidity for trading is ample especially for the major currencies. Liquidity allows the traders to buy and sell the currencies quickly at any time; there is a flow of traders in the market. A large number of participants in the market enable the trader to transact extremely large orders of currencies without diverting the prices too much. Liquidity reduces the chances of price anomalies and manipulation, and as such, the spreads become tighter leading to efficient pricing. A trader does not have to worry about the stagnant prices during the afternoon and high volatility during the opening and closing which constantly affect the equity markets. In the forex market, a trader can observe similarities in the patterns of volatility (low, mid and high) apart from times when major events occur.

Lack of a central exchange

Keeping in mind that the forex exchange market operates globally, there is no central regulatory or centralized exchange. The market operates as an over the counter although central banks occasionally interfere with the operations as needed in order to regulate it. However, it is very rare for the central banks of any other authority to intervene unless under extreme conditions. The decentralization and deregulation of the market ensure that the traders are safe from sudden surprises. Many of the other security markets are centralized for example the equity market. When a company trading in the equity market suddenly reports losses or declares a dividend, the prices suddenly react to the information. Regulated markets also have higher chances of insider information compared to forex markets.

A variety of currency pairs to trade

There are eight major currencies traded in the forex market, and they result in 28 major currency pairs that one may choose from. A trader can select any pair and easily switch from one to the other.

Low-capital requirements

A trader can start trading in the forex market with a low amount of initial capital because of the tight spread in relation to pips. In some other markets, one may not be able to trade without a large amount of capital. To ice the low capital cake, forex exchange also has a margin trading and leverage factor.

Technical strategy

Many traders venturing into bonds and equity have to delve deep into the financial and fundamental state of the bonds or share issuer in order to confirm that there are chances of making a profit. On the other hand, in the forex market, traders do not have to dig too deep, all they need is to study the price charts. Technical analysis of forex market price charts helps traders identify their entry and exit points. However, they may choose to combine technical and fundamental analysis when selecting a trade.

While fundamental analysis requires one to get detailed background information about the assets of the issuer and the financial health and prospects, Technical analysis requires one to watch the ongoing as well as the historical or repetitive market trends, therefore, gathering clues on the demands and supply of the currencies.

No insider price manipulation

Many markets such as stock markets and bond markets can be influenced by information held privately by some investors and insiders who have interests in the assets. This is because most of the markets are centralized. Foreign exchange markets are not centralized; therefore, they cannot be easily manipulated by people who have insider information.

In most cases, the only holders who can access insider information in the forex exchange are central bank authorities or government officials, and they are usually under a lot of intense scrutiny from the public and the private sectors. As such, the foreign exchange market is one of the most transparent markets one can trade in.

Few commissions and fees

Traders get charged Pricey commissions and hidden trading fees when dealing with bonds, equities mutual funds and other kinds of instruments. This makes trading very expensive and reduces the profits of the trader. In forex trade, the costs of trading are determined by the bid-ask price only. The spread price is the difference between the bid and the asking price which is clearly published in real time by the brokers. As such, a trader does not have to worry about eliminating breakage overheads. This aspect makes Forex exchange more advantageous to trade in.

Simple tax rules

In many other markets, the traders have to keep track of their trading activities both in the short term and the long term in order to report taxes. However Foreign exchange trading is in most cases subject to a simpler tax rule, therefore, making tax calculations very easy.

Automation

Technology advancements have made it easy for forex traders to trade with utmost ease. The trade has adapted well to automated trading strategies, and with some training, a trader can reap the benefits of the available moves. A trader can set up programming entry, automated trades, limit prices and stop loss before he/she even makes a trade. The trader may also instruct the trading platform to transact when there are certain price movements or market conditions.

When a trader identifies a well revised automated strategy, he/she may have the chance to take advantage of the daily swings in the market without having to put all their efforts in keeping up with the movements in the market.

Chapter 1. What Is Forex Trading? Overview and history of Forex Trading

Forex is a short form of Foreign Exchange, and therefore FOREX trading is the exchange of currencies around the world. It is a trade that is referred to as Over the Counter Trade (OTC) because it takes place without a physical place to meet. The buyer and the seller are only connected through telephone, telex, and a communication system. However, there are a few centers where the trade takes place in fixed places, an example is in Paris and Brussels, where bank representatives meet to bargain and fix rates of popular currencies. In FOREX trade, the major currencies include the US Dollar, the Japanese Yen, and the Euro. The participants in the trade include the central banks, exchange brokers, commercial banks, and corporate businesses. The individual traders are involved in the trade through exchange brokers.

The history of FOREX trading dates back to the end of World War II. After the war, the world started to experience economic instability, and most western governments needed to curb the situation. The government, therefore, agreed to have a Bretton Woods System, which was to exchange gold with other currencies. All the currencies were then traded against the US dollar that was set using the value of gold at the time. The situation stabilized for some time, but when the economies started growing at different paces, the system became limiting for major economies such as the US. The fluctuation rate was limited to a maximum or minimum of 1% compared to the dollar, and any nation that violated this had to control the imbalance through its central bank. The US eventually stopped using the Bretton Woods System, which brought a crisis that led to the abolishment of the system in 1971. The Bretton Woods System was replaced by another currency valuation system. The new system was different such that unlike the Bretton System, which had fixed rates, it had free-floating rates that were determined by the forces in the market. Individual currencies varied in value, thus increasing the need for exchange and trading. This system is what is still in use for FOREX exchange today. The new system had a problem of determining fair rates of exchange, but they were alleviated later, as the improvement in communication technology made it easier.

Earlier, the FOREX market was operated exclusively by central banks between governments and commercial banks. In the 1980s and 1990s, it was expanded to commodity trading advisors (CTAs), funds, big investors and large corporations. This is because this group of investors was able to adhere to the strict guidelines established for credit by the big banks; smaller investors could not meet the guidelines. In the 2000s, the market grew and gained much recognition by more individuals around the world. The computer technology also grew rapidly during this period, leading to the emergence of online FOREX trading, which is done through brokers.

The online FOREX brokers create a credit line with a bank that is involved in the trade to enable access to currencies for trade purposes. The trade now involves small volumes of currencies, contrary to the earlier trading system that required individuals to have large sums of money to trade in large volumes. Today, investors are more rigorous and seek to diversify their trading portfolios to draw more returns.

The FOREX trade is in the financial market together with stock trading and others. However, it is different from the other trades in the financial market, such that you do not need to use a centralized exchange that has only one price for a particular currency, at a given time. It is made up of different dealers that have different rates, making the market overwhelming, but amazing because it has so many choices. Competition between the many dealers is fierce, and getting the best deal is something that happens all the time. Another good thing about FOREX is that you can trade anywhere; you are not restricted to certain markets like in the case of stock trading.

The market has many dealers, as mentioned earlier, but they are organized on a ladder. At the top of the market, the ladder is interbank, which is composed of the world largest banks and some of the smaller banks. Traders at this level trade with each other directly through Reuters Dealing or the Electronic Brokerage Services (EBS). From the interbank going down the ladder, next is the hedge funds, retail market makers, and corporations; this group does its transactions through commercial banks, therefore their rates are higher than those of interbank. At the lower part of the ladder are the retail traders, who include individuals who are small scale traders.

FOREX trading is one of the trades that brings profits to a country; the more responsible traders a country has, the more it earns from the exchange. Entry in this form of trade is always a good choice of investment, as there are no trading commissions like other forms of trade. There are no government fees, exchange or clearing fees. There are also no brokerage fees as most brokers are compensated through the "spread." The only cost incurred is the transaction fee, which is low; it ranges from 0.07% to 0.1 where the lowest is for larger transactions. The FOREX trade also has no limit like in the case of stock and features, your size of the trade is determined by the amount of money you are willing to invest in the trade. FOREX is a 24-hour market; it does not have opening times or opening bells and does not depend on the day of the week or month, which makes it suitable for all people, including part-time traders. The market also attracts everyone because of its easy entry; when compared to other financial market trades, FOREX requires a minimum of $25 and allows individuals to have mini and micro-accounts for trading. The market welcomes all people, but no individual, institution, or company can control the market price, because it is so huge. This form of trade has high liquidity because the market is so huge and accessible that anytime you want to buy or sell; there is always someone willing to exchange.

When trading, one currency is exchanged with another, for instance, when you exchange Dollars with Euros, you say you are trading Dollars for Euros. The earning comes in when the money you traded with fluctuates in value over time. The rule is always to buy when it is low, and sell when it is high. However, it is not easy to determine how low is low and how high is high; to determine the low and high therefore one needs know the factors influencing the rate of the currency in order to predict the rate of the currency in the future. The difference between the rate of selling and that of buying a currency is known as the "spread" and it is expressed in "pips." A Pip is the smallest unit of any currency.

It is not easy to predict a market trend, and there are methods used to guide the prediction. These prediction methods are technical analysis and fundamental analysis. The fundamental analysis consists of analyzing policies put forth by a country that affect the currency. The central bank of each nation has the responsibility for a nation's well-being, and therefore, it analyses the factors that affect the economy and make policies aimed to improve the status of the economy. It is therefore important to constantly monitor regular announcements and policy adjustments the country of the currency you want to trade makes because they are the economic indicators that bring about changes in the FOREX market. The indicators include interest rates, the GDP, consumer price index, and industrial production, among others

The technical analysis concentrates on market trends, trying to see if the current trend of the currency can reverse, and if it does, how the market will respond to the changes in the future. It looks at the history of the price of currencies and volumes traded, through reading and interpreting graphs. Mathematical tools used in making technical analysis include gaps and trends, waves, and number theory. The technical analysis uses three basic assumptions: history repeats itself, prices move in trends and market discounts everything.

For one to have a reasonable profit from the FOREX trading it is good to have a good risk management plan. However, the management should be based on capital preservation; remember that you cannot trade without funds in your account. Making big profits is not bad, but it is good to take calculated risks. It is better to have a smaller success rate than to risk too much and lose it all.

An investor should also have a trading plan to make sure that he or she achieves the set goals. The plan should not just be written down, it should be followed just like you would if you were buying household items; always buy when the prices are low and when your prediction about the price increase has a higher chance of being true. On the other hand, sell when your prediction of a price decrease has a high probability of being correct and true. There is no proper action to FOREX trading; it all simply comes down to having a good plan based on a solid analysis.

Forex trading is not a trade that one can pull off without breaking a sweat before exchanging currencies. Before you make your first trade you need to study and thoroughly analyze the market patterns. Below you will find a list of things to need to study and to do before you start trading Forex and become a successful player.

Forex Trading Terminology

There are a lot of terms used that are new to a trader who is just starting off and are vocabularies to them. It would do well to an aspiring trader to acquaint themselves with the new terms and understand the meaning behind them and how to use them appropriately when trading. This will prove essential to avoid miscomprehension of certain concepts when trading. To new traders, the terms may be a little bit difficult and also have a completely different meaning than the expected one from its word-formation. The following words discussed below are some of the new vocabularies that will be encountered by a new trader, which are common in the language of trading.

A pip. A pip is the lowest measure of the value of movement of currency under observation. The term pip is, however, an abbreviation of the term-percentage in point. A pip, as the lowest measurable value of the movement that the currency makes, always measures ad 1% of the currency that a trader wants to exchange. When in the forex market a currency increases or decreases by a single pip, the inference has the meaning that the currency either increased or decreased by 1%. A great example is when the market analysis tools show that the US dollar has increased by a pip. This is to mean that the US dollar has increased in its value by $0.0001.

That is how a pip is inferred and its meaning. Trade is always made in terms of pips, and a trader can make trades with as many pips as possible. This is because the pips are the lowest value that is measured by the currency.

The base currency. The base currency is the type of currency that a trader has and is currently holding. The base currency is likely the currency of the country that you're from. If a trader is from the US, his or her base currency will be the US dollar. If the trader is from the UK, the base currency of the trader will be the pound. The base currencies of traders therefore different across many traders around the globe due to different geographical differences.

The asking price. The asking price is a term that is used to refer to the amount of money that your broker firm will demand from or will ask from you when you are making a trade. A broker always demands this price, or this amount of money when they are accepting the pair of currencies to be traded from you. The price id for buying the quote that you've made of the pair of currencies. A note to be made is that the asking price; made by the brokerage firms, is always higher than the bid price, as will be discussed immediately below.

Bid price. The bid price is mostly used in reference to the brokerage firms, where it is the amount of money that the brokers will be willing to buy or to bid the base currency that you are currently holding. The broker firm sets the bid price according to their ability to bid on the base currency that has.

Quote currency. The quote currency, unlike the base currency, is the currency that a trader wants and is willing to purchase, in exchange for his or her base currency. If a trader wants to exchange US dollars to get South African Rand, the currency of South Africa; the Rand is the quote currency. It is always stroked against the base currency when trading and when the currencies are made into pairs.

The spread. This is the commission that the broker firm receives from being a platform where forex trading can take place. When referred to, the spread means the difference in value between the bid price made by the broker and the asking price, also quoted by the broker.

These are but a few but the major terms that are used in the forex trading world. Knowing this alone will not be enough, you have to be familiar with more words and phrases that can be found in books concerning forex trading. Not only in books but also videos, forums and such where forex trading is discussed.

Finding the Right Broker Firm

So as to trade forex, you will have to have a brokerage firm that will be an online platform from which you'll open and close trade. Finding the right broker firm is an important process for other brokers can be a sham out to cheat people of their money. It is therefore paramount that a trader carries out research on the available broker firms and picks out the best and one that is highly recommended for its services. When deciding on which broker firm to go with, look at the ask and the bid price that the broker quotes, and other important aspects including the margin and the leverage level that they offer. The customer service should also be top-notch for the broker, which will be great for a trader who is just starting off. Most of the broker companies also offer studies on how to carry out forex trading and those come in handy to the new traders. Reviews by other forex traders is a great place to start on choosing the quality of a broker.

Making an Analysis of the Worldwide Economy

To make gains and profits and gains in trades that you are going to make, analyzing the economic trends of the worldwide economy is of great import to be fully aware of the factors that may trigger the currencies to increase or decrease in value. This is important in making a correct prediction on the pair of currencies you're exchanging, whether they will make a profit or a loss. Factors that are important to look into when evaluating the global economy are like the political climate of countries whose currencies have a strong value, natural factors that may influence the economy of countries, the Gross Domestic Product of the country whose currency you want to exchange with your base currency, and other minor factors such as the investment rate of the said country. Evaluating which countries are looking up to growth and development opportunities is also important in determining the quote currency to use impairing up currencies to make a trade. Also on the analysis of the worldwide economy, when the currency of the country you seek to purchase in exchange of your base currency is doing well and is set to increase in its value, convert your base currency into the quote currency. On the other hand, convert the quote currency into the base currency in case its value increases. There are various online sites that have analysis tools on the economic performance of different countries that you may seek for them to be your quote currency. Others rank counties in terms of their GDP that makes it easier for you to choose the countries that are projected for growth and development. Being in touch with the trending news globally is a plus in getting information relevant to trading forex. A new forex trader may subscribe to a few forex trading channels and outlets to be constantly on toes of events and happenings that may trigger the value of currencies to either increase or decrease, which may result in the reversal of the outlook of the trade made. Having relevant information at all times is key in making gains and preventing the loss of your money and probably your account is cleared.

Opening the First Trade

Pairing currencies and making the first trade; opening and closing a trade happens when the quote currency to be paired by the base currency have been paired and there is an opportune trading window. Opening a trade is making an order to purchase a certain currency and in exchange for your base current through your broker firm. You'll have the analysis tools, that are commonly offered by the brokers in software programs. The execution of making an order in some platforms might be instant while in some other platforms, it might be a tad bit slower. Nonetheless, most brokerage firms offer live prices and values of the currencies that are to traded and their exchange rates and the instant changes to their values are displayed. The first trade for a new trader might just be one or others might open up new trades over a short period of time. It is advisable that just several enough trades be opened, which the new trader is comfortable and at ease in trading.

Chapter 2. Which Currencies are There and Which are the Best Ones to Trade

Us Dollar (Usd)

To this day, the United States dollar remains the world's most important currency. This is particularly true in Forex. The strength of the US dollar has proven itself to be formidable, despite having gone through a lot of financial roadblocks instigated by local and global turmoil. The strength of the currency can be attributed to the country's continued economic strength. The United States has the largest economy, and the country does possess an abundant and liquid capital. Aside from its economy, the strength of the country's currency can also be attributed to its role in the global stage and might of its political and military presence.

The movements of all other currencies still pivot around the market's perception of the US dollar, making it the fulcrum of the Forex market. The US dollar is the most liquid amongst the other currencies, making it the only option to become the world's reserve currency. Around 65 percent of the world's reserves are in US dollars. Due to this fact, central banks around the world now choose to hold a massive amount of this particular currency within their ledgers.

Investors and businesses also regard the US dollar as the go-to safe currency. This has been proven during different global financial situations. During the global credit crisis in 2009, which caused the Lehman Brothers and Bear Stearns to go bankrupt, the US dollar actually appreciated in value. Investors who were fearful for the worst moved their assets to US government securities, which resulted in the currency's value increase. While most may not agree that treasury bonds are the safest location, what is important to note is that the US dollar is perceived as the safest investment in the world. As of the moment, the US dollar remains at the top in the Forex markets.

Euro (EUR)

While being relatively new on the global financial scene, the euro is currently the second most important currency in the Forex market. The currency was introduced in 1999 and officially entered circulation in 2002. The euro was meant to centralize the currencies of the different European countries, which mostly had their own currencies. Due to the proximity of the nations belonging to the European Union, a solution had to be made to eliminate unnecessary currency conversions. Over the years, it has completely replaced other sovereign currencies, including most recently the French franc and the Deutsche mark.

The euro is currently valued higher than a US dollar, and it has been able to keep it that way since it was introduced. The euro has also much appreciated in value by more than 70 percent since 2002. Investors and traders who bet big on its rise certainly made a lot of profit during that time. Over the years, a lot of confidence has also been put on the currency, making it a good alternative. Similar to other currencies, the euro has had its own share of ups and downs, particularly during the global credit crisis in 2008. The euro peaked at US$ 1.60 during that year. The global credit crisis wreaked havoc on the European banking system. The situation got worse, and the European Central Bank had to intervene. Several members of the European Union were on the verge of bankruptcy. Portugal, Ireland, Greece, and Spain all received financial support from the IMF and the European Union to avoid defaulting on their debt.

Japanese Yen (Jpy)

The Japanese yen has been one of the most successful stories in modern foreign exchange. Japan's recovery after World War II saw it emerge as a formidable economic force on the world stage. Since the yen's introduction to the work market, it has grown by a staggering 400 percent against the US dollar. The rise started with the initial economic boom in Japan and is continuing up to this day. Japan is currently one of the world's second-largest economies, and it was holding that position until China overtook it.

The growth of the Japanese yen has unfortunately halted by the early 1990s. However, it has managed to stay at the same relative value. Price inflation in the country has not been a problem in the country, partly thanks to its sophisticated financial system. Japan currently has one of the largest debts in work, on a per-capita basis, but it continues to enjoy healthy demand for its currency. The country continues to attract large investments from all over the world. The performance of the Japanese yen and the country itself is quite impressive given that it does not have a lot of natural resources. The country mostly gets its commodities and energy needs from other nations.

In the last decade, the value of the yen had slightly declined. This was mainly caused by extremely low-interest rates in Japan, which some investors had taken full advantage of by taken out loans and making investments abroad. The decline was halted when investors decided to let go of their short bets on the currency.

British Pound (Gbp)

The British pound, or the pound sterling, is currently the fourth-most-traded currency. Prior to the rise of the US Dollar, it was the strongest currency in the world. The strength of the British pound can be attributed to the fact that London remains to be the preeminent currency trading center in the world. Post-World War II, the British pound had gone through quite the fluctuations. Most of the dips can be attributed to the country's continually rising inflation and unemployment levels. The country's housing market is also nowhere near as robust as other countries. The United Kingdom's debt is also quite substantial, and its decision to print more money only made it worse.

Swiss Franc (Chf)

Switzerland is amongst the wealthiest countries in the world, and its economy is robust and has proven itself to be very stable. Due to this fact, the Swiss franc has become the go-to currency for those looking for an excellent place to store their finances. The economy's stability is mostly thanks to the country's trade surplus and its profitable exports. This includes the export of highly-valuable jewelry such as expensive Swiss watches, tobacco products, chemicals, and manufacturing equipment. Switzerland also mostly evaded the effects of the global credit crisis thanks to the Swiss National Bank's decision to refrain from printing money.

Similar to the US dollar, the Swiss franc is a safe-haven currency. Some would even argue that it performs better than the US dollar in this regard. In fact, during times of global financial uncertainty, the value of the Swiss franc typically increases more than the other "safe" currencies. As for its movement in the Forex market, the Swiss franc closely mirrors the movement of the euro. This is mostly due to the close relationship with the Swiss and the Eurozone economies. However, the currency's value does deviate in times of political strife, thanks mainly to the country's neutrality in global political issues.

Australian Dollar (Aud)

While it might not sound correct, the Australian dollar is actually one of the strongest commodity currencies in the market. Its movement is closely tied to the movement of global commodity prices. This is mainly since the country is one of the world's largest producers of iron ore, coal, and other precious metals. The country's economy has so far taken advantage of China's growing demand for energy and basic commodities. Thanks to this, the country's economy was really damaged by the recent global financial crisis. Due to its close trade relationship with Asian countries, especially China, the Australian dollar's movement does somewhat mirror that of the Chinese yuan. In fact, some investors even treat the currency as a good proxy for the Chinese yuan.

Canadian Dollar (Cad)

The Canadian dollar is another commodity currency that is closely related to global commodity prices. The country is a large producer of energy commodities such as petroleum, timber, and coal. It also exports a number of agricultural products to different parts of the world. The Canadian dollar took advantage of the commodities boom in the mid-2000s and gained in 2010 where its value equaled that of the US dollar. This was the very first time that the Canadian dollar reached parity with the US dollar in over 30 years. Canada's economy is greatly dependent on that of the United States. Canada produces oil, electricity, and natural gas for the United States, which purchases around 75 percent of what the country produces. When the United States experiences a downtrend in its economy, the Canadian dollar swiftly follows.

Other Currencies

There are currently around 180 legal currencies that are circulating throughout the world. Amongst those currencies, only a handful are actively traded on the Forex market. Most Forex brokers trade between 40 to 70 currency pairs, with some trading more than others. Aside from the currencies mentioned above, there are a few currencies that have become recently significant. This includes the New Zealand dollar, which is closely influenced by the movement of the Australian dollar. The New Zealand dollar is also greatly reliant on the prices of global commodities. The country is a large producer of agricultural products and dairy-based items. The Chinese Yuan has also recently gained prominence, thanks to the rapid growth of the country's economy. It is arguably a currency that investors should look out for given its sudden emergence into the world stage. China has the second largest economy in the world, and it is one of the biggest international traders out there. The Chinese Yuan is pinned to the US dollar.

Apart from the major currencies mentioned above and the recent ones that have gained prominence, all of the other currencies are considered to be exotic currencies. These currencies are also sometimes referred to as emerging market currencies; mostly due to their association with their respective country's emerging economies. These economies tend to have large fluctuations in the market, mostly due to high inflation and significant political and economic changes. In some cases, some of these currencies can rise to unprecedented levels when times are good. However, these are also the currencies that drop the most during times of crisis. Some of the more popular exotic currencies that are traded in the Forex market include the Korean won (KRW), Turkish lira

(TRY), the Russian ruble (RUB), the Indian rupee (INR), the Brazilian real (BRL) and the South African Rand (ZAR). Along with seven other exotic currencies, these emerging currencies account for a combined 9 percent overall trade volume in the Forex market.

Currency Pairs

Among the 160 different currencies circulating in different parts of the world, there are only handfuls that are actively exchanged in the Forex market. Most of them are only exchanged in the territories where they are used. The current Forex market actively trades in only around 17 currencies based on their liquidity and the number of exchanges made between those currencies. These so-called major currencies account for over 90 percent of all the money exchanged in the foreign currency exchange market.

Similar to company stocks in the stock market, currencies are assigned three-letter abbreviations, set by the International Standards Organization. This greatly simplifies the quoting and trading of these currencies in the world market. When trading these currencies, the quote for these trades is always shown in pairs. Each currency fluctuates relative to other currencies, which is why they are traded in pairs. Out of the active major currencies, there are hundreds of potential currency combinations. However, there are about 100 pairs that are commonly traded, with around 50 pairs actively being used by international Forex brokers.

In Forex trading, exotic currencies are generally paired with major currencies. It is doubtful that a non-major currency will be paired with another non-major currency. As an example, it would be challenging to find an exchange that trades the Uruguay Peso and the Iraqi dinar. However, finding an exchange that trades those currencies with the US dollar is relatively easy. Some companies and individuals do exotic trade pairs with another, but their volume merely is just too small for international brokers.

Currency Quotations

The International Organization for Standardization submitted ISO 4217 in 1978. The standard assigned three-letter codes to represent individual currencies to be used in any application for trading, banking, and commerce. It was also agreed upon that the three-letter alphabetic codes for International Standard ISO 4217 would be used in international trading. The list of codes is also frequently updated, as new currencies emerge and older ones are discontinued.

When it comes to Forex trading, currencies always come in pairs. As an example, a trade made with the US dollar versus the euro would look like this (USD/EUR). The US dollar versus the Canadian dollar would look like this (USD/CAD). It goes without saying that a currency can never be traded without itself.

The first currency indicated in the quotation is called the base currency, while the second one is referred to as the counter currency. A numerical value is assigned to the currency pair that may be up to 4 decimal places. The last decimal place is referred to as a "pip." The value assigned to currency pairs is the amount of the counter currency required to buy one unit of the base currency. As an example, if the USD/CAD is quoted at 1.32, it means that it would currently require 1.32 Canadian dollars to buy one single US dollar. On trading platforms, these values would fluctuate in real-time as the value of each currency varies depending on the market.

Chapter 3.   Who Can Trade On the Forex Market?

A broker refers to a firm or somewhat an individual who charges a certain fee or rather a commission for executing the buying and the selling process. In other words, they play the role of connecting the customer and the seller of the product. Thus, they are generally paid for acting as a link between the two parties. For instance, a client might be willing to buy shares from a particular organization. However, he might be lacking enough information about the places that he can purchase these shares. Thus, he will be forced to seek a person who understands well the stock exchange markets. The broker will, therefore, educate the client as well as link them with the right sellers. The broker will thus earn by offering such a connection. Other brokers sell insurance policies to individuals. In most cases, the individuals earn a commission once the clients they brought in the organization buy or renews the system. Any insurance companies have utilized the aspect as a way of increasing their sales.

List of Common Brokers

IG

It is rated as one of the best forex brokers in the world. It was one of the pioneers in offering contracts for difference as well as spread beating. The organization was founded in the year 1974 and had been growing as a leader in online trading as well as the marketing industry. One of the aspects that have boosted its growth is the fact that it has linked a lot of customers, hence gaining more trust. In other words, a duet to its large customer base, a lot of clients prefers selling and buying their services. The other aspect worth noting is that this organization is London based, and it is among one of the companies that are listed on the London Stock Exchange market for more than 250 times. The aspect is due to the fact that it offers more than 15,000 products across several asset classes. Such classes include CFDs on shares, forex, commodities, bonds, crypto currencies as well as indices. Another aspect worth noting is that the 2019 May report, the firm is serving more than 120,000 active clients around the globe. Also, there are more than 350,000 clients that are served on a daily basis. The aspect has been critical in boosting its expansion as this group of individuals does more advertisements.

Some of the benefits that one gains by working in this industry are the fact that it allows comprehensive trading and the utilization of tools that enhance the real exchange of data. The other aspect worth noting is that it has a public traded license that allows a regular jurisdiction across the entire globe. In other words, one can acquire the services of this organization across the whole world with ease without the fear of acting against the laws of the nation. Also, the premises offer some of the competitive based commission that enhances pricing as spreading of forex. There is also a broad range of markets that are associated with the premises too, there several currencies and multi assets CFDs that are offered by the organization. The aspect has been critical in the sense that it allows the perfect utilization of all the services as well as the resources available across the globe. Some of the services that are offered by the organization are permitted globally, such that even after traveling from one nation to the other, one can still access their services. Since the year 1974, the organization has joined more than 195,000 traders across the entire globe. The aspect has allowed the selling its shares as well as services hence its fame.

Saxo Bank

The forex broker was established in 1992and has then been among the leading organization in offering forex services as well as the multi-asset brokerages across more than 15 nations. Some of these nations include the UK, Denmark, and Singapore, among others. One of the aspects of the organization is that it offers services to both retailers as well as institutional clients in the globe. The character has allowed the premises to provide more than one million transactions each day. Thus, it holds over $ 16 billion in asset management. The Saxo bank also offers more services to all of her clients. Such services include Spot FX, Non-deliverable Forwards (NDFs), contract difference as well as all the stock exchange options. The aspect has been critical in increasing its customer base across the globe. Some of the services such as crypto and bond services that are offered in the premises has allowed its expansion in the sense that they are sensitive and essentials.

Some of the benefits that one gain by assessing the services of the premises are that it enhances diverse selection of quality, it increases competitive commissions and forex spread as well as an improved multiple financial jurisdiction function that is allowed across the entire globe. In other words, the premises offer services that are allowed in the whole world, and that considers the rules and policies provided in each nation. The aspect has enhanced its continued growth despite the increased competition. One is required to pay a minimum deposit of about $2000 and an automated trading solution for all the traders. There are times when the premises offer bonuses of 182 trade forex pairs to all its clients. The aspect has also been the key reason behind its increased expansion. In other words, there are various services offered at a relatively low price hence the widening of its customer base.

CMC Markets

The premises were founded in 1989 and since then, it has grown to be one of the leading retail forex as well as a CFD brokerage. The premises thus serve more than 10,000 CFD instruments that cut across all the classes such as forex, commodities as well as security markets. The aspect has allowed the premises to spread its services to more than 60,000 clients across the entire globe. The premises have more than 15 offices that are well distributed in the nation; it offers the services. Most of its actions are thus related in UK, Australia as well as Canada. The aspect is due to the fact that the premises have it is customer bases in some of these nations. In other words, its serves are well are accepted in Canada and the UK.

There are various benefits that one gains by joining the premises. One, the premise offers some of the best competitive spread to all her customers. In other words, there are a variety of services that one can choose from. Also, the premises offer some of the largest selection of currency pairs in the entire industry. There are more than one hundred and eighty currencies that one can access by joining the premises. The other aspect worth noting is that the premises offer some of the best regulated financial agents in the entire globe. In other words, there are policies as well as rules that govern the provision of services in the world. Also, it is easy to identify the premises as there are potent charts as well as patterns that are used as recognition tools.

City Index

The forex broker was founded in 1983 in the UK. Since then, the premises have gained popularity and has turned out to be one of the leading brokers in London. It is worth noting that in 2015, the premises acquired GAIN Capital Holding Company that enhanced its increased customer base. Since 2015, the premises have been providing traders with services such as CFDs and spreading-betting derivatives. The premises have been further expanding the forex services with the acquisition of markets as well as FX solutions before gaining the capital market. Nowadays, the City Index has been operating as an independent brand under GAIN Capital in Asia as well as the UK. The aspect has allowed a multi-asset solution hence offering traders access to over 12,000 products across the global markets.

Some of the benefits that one gains part of the capital holding, a large selection of CFDs as well as regulated in several jurisdictions. The organization has tight spreads as well as low margins and fast execution. In others, the premises have been time from time, offering average ranges to all the clients; hence its increased customer base.

XTB Review

The organization was founded in Poland in the year 2002. Since then the organization has been well known for its forex and CFDs brokerage. Since then, the organization has maintained its offices in several nations; it offers its services. The premise has been working as a multi-asset broker that is regulated in several centers, hence increasing their competitive advantage. The premises have been trading as multiple financial centers offering a lot of services to all her traders. With a wide range of more than 2000 functions, the premises have been trading in almost all nations hence an increase in its customer base. The premises also offer excellent services that have been the reason behind its expansion. One of the aspects that have made the forex broker be thriving in such a competitive environment.

Choosing Of A Broker And A Trading Platform

It is appropriate that you chose a reputable broker. I advise that as a beginner, start by taking a considerable amount of time to do deep research on the differences between the available brokers. Try to understand the different policies that each broker has as well as how each of these brokers goes about making a market. You have to understand that doing trade in the over-the-counter market differs from exchange driven market. Again, I advise that you be sure of the trading platform your broker is using so as to know the suitable analysis that will fit you. For instance, if you trade by analyzing Fibonacci numbers, just ensure that the platform your broker is using also supports the drawing of Fibonacci lines. Try to figure out good brokers with poor trading platforms, poor brokers with good trading platforms and good brokers with good trading platforms. Ensure that you choose a good broker with a good trading platform.

Signs of Illegitimate Brokers

Although numerous brokers have been working in the Forex industry, the aspect of legitimacy has been an issue affecting the progress of some these businesses. One of the elements that are considered is the vulnerability of the clients. In most cases illegitimate brokers tend to rob of their customers. Most of them are self-reliant and optimistic. Most of them operate above their financial knowledge, hence making numerous mistakes. Most of these organization record big loses as they are relatively weak in term of management. The organization offers a lot of transactions that tend to be cumbersome in terms of management. It is worth noting that most of their operations aren't legitimate and never approved by the necessary authorities. Thus, when deciding on the kind of forex broker to seek services from, it is essential to consider some factors. Avoid assumptions that are exaggerative in terms of offering services that are above their knowledge. The aspect is harmful in the sense that they provide services that are not well planned hence recording a number of losses that befalls many clients in the long run.

Here are some things to look out for.

Distrust cold calls

Distrust any broker or investment advisor who contacts you unsolicited representing a company with which you've never done business. These "cold calls" could take the form of a phone call, email or letter. Don't get fooled by invitations to seminars promising free lunches or other gifts in order to get you to lower your guard and invest blindly. Be especially suspicious of those who use high-pressure sales tactics, once-in-a-lifetime opportunities or refuse to send written information about an investment.

Call Them, Have a Chat with Them

If you're going to do business and invest your money with these people you need to feel comfortable and be sure everything is in order. Ask lots of questions, and find out what relationship you are going to have with the firm or your broker. Under a fiduciary standard, brokers and advisors must put their client's interest above and before their own when suggesting investments, while under the so called suitability standard, the professional is only required to make suggestions consistent with the client's best interests. Investment advisors must always follow the fiduciary standard, broker-dealers don't have to.

If they are not willing to give straight answers or sound overly evasive, find another broker/advisor.

Test their reputation, do some research

Start off by searching the broker and firm name on the web. You could find news releases, media reports of alleged wrongdoing and disciplinary actions, customer conversations on forums, background info, and such. Watch out for complaints from customers about not being able to withdraw funds. Try typing "Bernie Madoff" and see the thousands of results that brings up.

Regularly Check Your Statements

In order to help you detect wrongdoings, or mistakes check your statements carefully on a regular basis. If the investment returns don't meet your expectations or there are unforeseen changes in your portfolio ask questions. Don't settle for overly complicated explanations you don't understand. If you don't get straight answers, get in touch with someone higher up. Don't be afraid to look ignorant or to be considered annoying.

Withdraw Your Funds and File a Complaint

If you suspect any misconduct, immediately withdraw funds. Once your money is safe, file a complaint with federal and private regulators.

Read Carefully the Fine Print Before Opening Your Account

Be sure you understand all conditions regarding incentives and withdrawals and make sure they are in your favor and not against you.

Start Small and Try the Broker Out

Give the broker a try for a month or so using a small amount of capital. Try to make a withdrawal. If all goes well and nothing negative comes out on your online searches, you can start thinking about scaling up operations.

Signs of Legitimate Brokers

Although there are numerous scams in the business, there are many legitimate forex brokers offering excellent services.

One good sign is the fact a particular broker has withstood the test of time and has a solid reputation. In a nutshell, when selecting a forex broker, it is good to consider several factors. It is critical to find out whether the broker is certified by some kind of national regulatory body or if has no regulation and if it has a good overall reputation with their customers.

For US brokers, you could check if the firm or broker is CFTC-registered. In order to know if a US forex broker is CFTC-registered and regulated by the NFA, the first step is to identify the NFA ID number from the disclosure text at the bottom of the broker's US homepage. For example, here's the key disclosure text from FOREX.com's website.

"FOREX.com is a registered FCM and RFED with the CFTC and member of the National Futures Association (NFA # 0339826)"

It is also a good idea to take into account the number of services as well as the types of transactions offered by the firm. Most of the illegitimate brokers tend to provide numerous poorly managed services. The customer reviews you find online are to be taken seriously into account as they reflect whether the brokers are legitimate or not. You should also consider taking a look, if possible, at the financial reports of these organizations. This would show at a glance if the brokers are making losses or profits on the market. Last but not least, if you are a US national, make sure the broker you choose accepts US customers, since not all of them do.

Here is the URL to a website listing registered and unregistered Forex brokers. Remember to do your research before committing to any of them and opening an account. https://www.forexchurch.com/forex-brokers?page=1

Chapter 4. Different Existing Trading Styles According to Personal Taste And/Or Available Portfolio

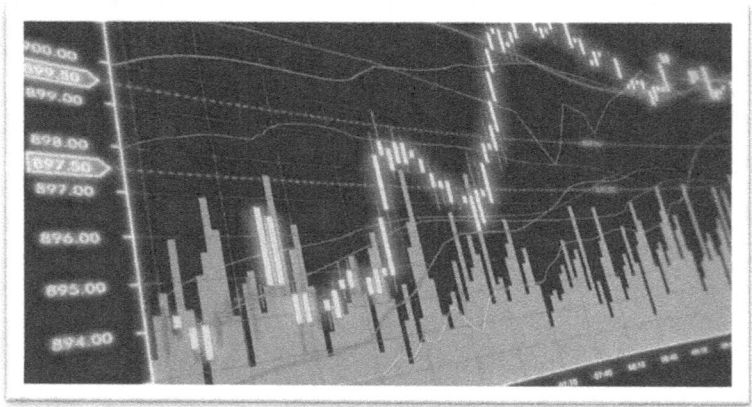

Forex Trading strategy is what forex traders do to buy or sell financial instruments at a given time to generate profits. Forex Trading strategies are nowadays done, either manually or automatically. A trader is using manual strategies when he or she interprets the trading signals and as a result, decides to buy or sell. The automated method is where a trader comes up with an algorithm that studies the trading signals and executes trades on its own.

Before choosing a Forex Trading strategy, it is important to identify which of these four trading styles fits your personality:

Day Trading

Day trading is a short-term trading style designed to buy and sell financial securities within the same trading day. That is closing all positions by the end of the trading day. In Day Trading, you can hold your trades for minutes or even hours. Day traders deal with financial instruments like options, stock, currencies, and contracts for difference. Many day traders are investment firms and banks. Day traders use technical analysis to make trading decisions.

Pros

- Day traders are not affected by unmanageable risks and negative price gaps because all positions are closed by the end of the trading day.
- There are a substantial number of trading opportunities
- Traders can be extremely profitable due to the rapid returns

Cons

- Traders can be extremely unprofitable due to the rapid returns
- You don't have to be concerned with the economy or long-term trends

- Huge opportunity cost
- Day traders have to exit a losing position very quickly, to prevent a greater loss.

Swing Trading

Swing trading is where a trader holds an asset between one and several days in an attempt to capture gains in the financial market. This type of traders doesn't monitor the screens all day, and they do it a few hours a day. Swing traders usually rely on technical analysis to look for trading opportunities. Swing trading position is held longer than day trading position but shorter than buy and hold investments. They have larger profit targets than day traders.

Pros

- Swing traders can rely solely on technical analysis, which simplifies the process
- Requires less time to trade compared to day-trading

Cons

- Swing traders are exposed to overnight and weekend risks
- Generally, swing trading risks are as a result of market speculation
- It is difficult to know when to enter and exit a trade when swing trading

Scalping Trading

Scalping is the fastest trading style where traders hold positions for a very short time frame. Traders here gain profits due to small price changes. The scalpers hold a position for a short period to gain profits. Traders with large amounts of capital or bid-offers spread narrowly prefer scalping. Scalping follows four principles:

Small moves are more frequent - even when the market is quiet, scalpers can make hundreds or thousands of trades

Small moves are easier to obtain - small moves happen all the time compared to large ones

Less risky than larger moves - scalpers only hold positions for short periods therefore because they have less exposure the risk is also lower

Spreads can be both bonuses and costs. Spread is the numerical difference between the bid and ask prices. Various parties and different strategies view spread as either trading bonuses or costs.

Pros

- Positions can be liquidated quickly, usually within minutes or seconds
- Very profitable when used as a primary strategy
- It's a low-risk strategy
- Scalpers are not exposed to overnight risks

Cons

- Requires an exit strategy especially during large losses
- Not the best strategy for beginners; it involves quick decision-making abilities.

Position Trading

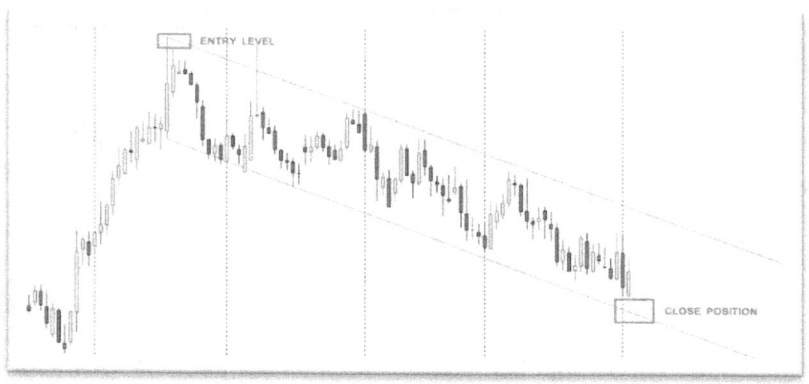

Position trading involves holding a position open for a long period expecting it to appreciate. Traders here can hold positions for weeks, months, or even years. Position traders are not concerned with short-term fluctuations; they are keener on long-term views that affect their positions. Position trading is not done actively. Most traders place an average of 10 trades a year.

This strategy seeks to capture full gains of long-term trading, which would result in an appreciation of their investment capital. Position traders use fundamental analysis, technical analysis, or a combination of both to make trading decisions. To succeed position, traders need plans in place to control risk as well as identify the entry and exit levels.

Pros

- Traders have a longer period to reap fruits.
- Trader's time is not on demand. Once the trade has been initiated, all they can do is wait for the desired outcome

Cons

- Traders may fall victim to opportunity costs because capital is usually tied up for longer periods.
- Position traders tend to ignore minor fluctuations, which can turn to trend reversals, a change in the price direction of a position.

Forex Trading Strategies

There are several types of forex strategies; however, it is important to choose the right one based preferred trading style to trade successfully. Some strategies work on short-term trades as well as long-term trades. The type of Forex strategies you choose depends on a few factors like:

- Entry points - traders need to determine the appropriate time to enter the market
- Exit point-trader need to develop rules on when to exit the market as well as how to get out of a losing position
- Time availability
- If you have a full-time job, then you cannot use day trading or scalping styles
- Personal choices

People who prefer lower winning rates but larger gains should go for position trading while those who prefer higher winning rate but smaller gains can choose the swing trading

Common Forex Trading strategies include:

Range Trading Strategy

Range trading is one of the many viable trading strategies. This strategy is where a trader identifies the support and resistance levels and buys at the support level and sells at the resistance level. This strategy works when there is a lack of market direction or the absence of a trend. Range trading strategies can be broken down into three steps:

Finding the Range

Finding the range uses the support and resistance zones. The support zone is the buying price of the security while the resistance zone price is the selling price of a security. A breakout happens in the event that the price goes beyond the trading range, whereas a breakdown occurs in the event that the price goes below the trading range.

Time Your Entry

Traders use a variety of indicators like price action and volume to enter and exit the trading range. They can also use oscillators like CCI, RSI, and stochastics to time their entry. The oscillators track prices using mathematical calculations. Then the traders wait for the prices to reach the support or resistance zones. They often strike when the momentum turns price in the opposing direction.

Managing Risk

The last step is risk management. When the level of support or resistance breaks, traders will want to exit any range-based positions. They can either use a stop loss above the previous high or invert the process with a stop below the current low.

Pros

- There are ranges that can last even for years producing multiple winning trades.

Cons

- Long-lasting ranges are not easy to come by, and when they do, every range trader wants to use it.
- Not all ranges are worth trading

Trend Trading Strategy

Another popular and common Forex Trading strategy is the trend trading strategy. This strategy attempts to make profits by analyzing trends. The process involves identifying an upward or downward trend in a currency price movement and choosing trade entry and exit points based on the currency price within the trend.

Trend traders use these four common indicators to evaluate trends; moving averages, relative strength index (RSI), On-Balance-Volume (OBV), and Moving Average Convergence Divergence (MACD). These indicators provide trend trade signals, warn of reversals, and simplify price information. A trader can combine several indicators to trade.

Pros

- Offers a better risk to reward
- Can be used across any markets

Cons

- Learning to trade on indicators can be challenging.

Pairs Trade

This is a neutral trading strategy, which allows pair traders to gain profits in any market conditions. This strategy uses two key strategies:

Convergence trading - this strategy focuses on two historically correlated securities, where the trader buys one asset forward and sells a similar asset forward for a higher price anticipating that prices will become equal. Profits are made when the underperforming position gains value, and the outperforming position's price deflates

Statistical trading - this is a short-term strategy that uses the mean reversion models involving broadly diversified Security Portfolios. This strategy uses data mining and statistical methods.

Pros

- If pair trades go as expected investors can make profits

Cons

- This strategy relies on a high statistical correlation between two securities, which can be a challenge.
- Pairs trade relies a lot on historical trends, which do not depict future trends accurately.

Price Action Trading

This Forex Trading strategy involves analyzing the historical prices of securities to come up with a trading strategy. Price action trading can be used in short, medium, and long periods. The most commonly used price action indicator is the price bar, which shows detailed information like high and low-price levels during a specific period. However, most traders use more than one strategy to recognize trading patterns, stop-losses, and entry, and exit levels. Technical analysis tools also help price action traders make decisions.

Pros

- No two traders will interpret certain price action the same way

Cons

- Past price history cannot predict future prices accurately

Carry Trade Strategy

Carry trade strategy involves borrowing a low-interest currency to buy a currency that has a high rate; the goal is to make a profit with the interest rate difference. For example, one can buy currency pairs like the Japanese yen (low interest) and the Australian dollar (high interest) because the interest rate spreads are very high. Initially, carry trade was used as a one-way trade that moved upwards without reversals, but carry traders soon discovered that everything went downhill once the trade collapsed.

With the carry trade strategy:

You need to first identify which currencies offer high rates and which ones have low rates.

Then match two currencies with a high-interest differential

Check whether the pair has been in an upward tendency favoring the higher-interest rate currency

Pros

- The strategy works in a low volatility environment.
- Suitable for a long-term strategy

Cons

- Currency rates can change anytime
- Ricky because they are highly leveraged
- Used by many traders therefore overcrowded

Momentum Trading

This strategy involves buying and selling assets according to the strength of recent price trends. The basis for this strategy is that an asset price that is moving strongly in a given direction will continue to move in the same direction until the trend loses strength. When assets reach a higher price, they tend to attract many investors and traders who push the market price even higher. This continues until large pools of sellers enter the market and force the asset price down. Momentum traders identify how strong trends are in a given direction. They open positions to take advantage of the expected price change and close positions when the prices go down.

There are two kinds of momentum:

Relative momentum - different securities within the same class are compared against each other, and then traders and investors buy strong performing ones and sell the weak ones.

Absolute momentum - an asset's price is compared against its previous performance.

Pros

- Traders can capitalize on volatile market trends
- Traders can gain high profit over a short period
- This strategy can take advantage of changes in stock prices caused by emotional investors.

Cons

- A momentum investor is always at a risk of timing a buy incorrectly.
- This strategy works best in a bull market; therefore, it is market sensitive
- This strategy is time-intensive; investors need to keep monitoring the market daily.

- Prices can shift in a different direction anytime

Pivot Points

This strategy determines resistance and support levels using the average of the previous trading sessions, which predict the next prices. They take the average of the high, low, and closing prices. A pivot point is a price level used to indicate market movements. Bullish sentiment occurs when one trades above the pivot point while bearish sentiment occurs when one trades below the pivot point.

Pros

- Traders can use the levels to plan out their trading in advance because prices remain the same throughout the day
- Works well with other strategies

Cons

- Some traders do not find pivot points useful
- There is no guarantee that price will stop or reverse at the levels created on the chart

Fundamental Analysis

This strategy involves analyzing the economic, social, and political forces that may affect the supply and demand of an asset. Usually, people use supply and demand to gauge which direction the price is headed to. The Fundamental analysis strategy then analyzes any factors that may affect supply and demand. By assessing these factors, traders can determine markets with a good economy and those with a bad one.

Forex Strategies For Beginners

When starting on Forex Trading, it important to keep things simple. As a beginner, avoid thinking about money too much and focus on one or two strategies at a time. The following three strategies are easy to understand and perfect for beginners.

Inside Bar Trading Strategy

This highly effective strategy is a two-bar price action strategy with an inside bar and a prior/mother bar. The inside bar is usually smaller and within the high and low range of the prior bar. There are many variations of the inside bar, but what remains constant is that the prior bar always fully engulfs the inside bar. Although very profitable, the inside bar setup does not occur often.

There are two main ways you can trade using inside bars:

- As a continuation move - This is the easiest way to trade inside bars. The inside bars are traded in trending markets following the direction of the trend.
- As a reversal pattern - the inside bars are traded counter-trend

- When using this strategy, it is important to look for these characteristics when evaluating the pattern:
- Time frame matters - avoid any time frame less than the daily.
- Focus on the breakout - best inside bar trades happen after a break of consolidation where the preceding trend is set to resume.
- The trend is your friend - trading with the trend is the only way to trade an inside bar
- A favorable risk to reward ratio is needed when trading an inside bar
- The size of the inside bar in comparison to the prior bar is extremely important

Pin Bar Trading Strategy

This strategy is highly recommended for beginners because it is easy to learn due to a better visual representation of price action on a chart. It is one of the easiest strategies to trade. Pin bars show a reversal in the market and, therefore, can be useful in predicting the direction of the price. Pin bars consist of one price bar, known as a candlestick price bar, which represents a sharp reversal and rejection of price. Candlestick charts are the clearest at showing price action.

There are various ways traders trading with pin bars can enter the market:

- At the current market price
- Using an on-stop entry
- At limit entry, which is at the 50% retrace of the pin bar

To improve your odds when using the pin bar strategy:

- Trade with the trend
- Wait for a break of structure
- Trade from an area of value

Some of the mistakes pin bar traders should avoid include the following:

- Assuming the market will reverse because of a pin bar
- Focus too much on the pin bars and miss out on other trading opportunities
- All pin bars are not the same and should not be treated as such

Forex Breakout Strategy

A breakout strategy is where investors find stocks that have built strong support or resistance level, wait for a breakout, and enter the market when momentum is in their favor. This strategy is important because it can offer expansions in volatility, major price moves, and limited risk. A breakout occurs when the price moves beyond the support or resistance level. The breakout strategy is good for beginners because they can catch every trend in the market. Breakouts occur in all types of market environments.

Traders establish a bullish position when prices are set to close above a resistance level and a bearish position when prices close below a support level. Sometimes traders can be caught on a false breakout, and the only way to determine if it is a false breakout is to wait for confirmation. False breakout prices usually go beyond the support and resistance level; however, they return to a prior trading range by the end of the day.

Good investors plan how they will exit the markets before establishing a position. With breakouts, there are two exit plans:

Where to exit with profit-traders can assess the stock recent behaviors to determine reasonable objectives. When traders meet their goals, they can exit the position. They can either raise a stop-loss to lock in profits or exit a portion of the position to let the rest run

Where to exit with a loss - breakout trading show traders clearly when a trade has failed, and therefore they can determine where to set stop-loss order. Traders can use the old support or resistance level to close a losing trade

Pros

- You can catch every trend in the market
- Prices can quickly move in your favor

Cons

- Traders can get caught in a false breakout
- It can be difficult to enter a trade

Tips for trading breakouts:

- Never sell on breakdown or buy on breakout both carry extreme risks
- Trade with the trend
- Wait for higher volume to confirm a breakout
- Take advantage of volatility cycles
- Enter on the retest of support or resistance
- Have a predetermined exit plan

Note

Beginners are more likely to be successful in trade than their experienced counterparts are because they have not yet cultivated any bad habits. Experienced traders have to break bad habits and put aside any emotions built over the years.

Chapter 5. What Is Fundamental Analysis?

In order to trade in the forex market successfully, one of the most important things you can learn is the most reliable way to spot a trade that is going to end up being reliably profitable from one that blows up in your face. This is where proper analysis comes in handy, whether technical or fundamental. Fundamental analysis is easier to learn, though it is more time consuming to use properly, while technical analysis can be more difficult to wrap your mind around but can be done quite quickly once you get the hang of it. While both will help you to find the information you are looking for, they go about doing so in different ways; fundamental analysis concerns itself with looking at the big picture while technical analysis focuses on the price of a given currency in the moment to the exclusion of all else.

This divide when it comes to information means that fundamental analysis will always be useful when it comes to determining currencies that are currently undervalued based on current market forces. The information that is crucial to fundamental analysis is generated by external sources which means there won't always be new information available at all times

Generally speaking, fundamental analysis allows you a likely glimpse at the future of the currency in question based on a variety of different variables such as publicized changes to the monetary policy that the countries you are interested in might affect. The idea here is that with enough information you can then find currency pairs that are currently undervalued because the market hasn't yet had the time to catch up with the changes that have been made. Fundamental analysis is always made up of the same set of steps which are described in detail below.

Start by determining the baseline: When it comes to considering the fundamental aspects of a pair of currencies, the first thing that you are going to want to do is to determine a baseline from which those currencies tend to return to time and again compared to the other commonly traded currency pairs. This will allow you to determine when it is time to make a move as you will be able to easily pinpoint changes to the pair that are important enough to warrant further consideration.

In order to accurately determine the baseline, the first thing you will need to do is to look into any relevant macroeconomic policies that are currently affecting your currency of choice. You will also want to look into the available historical data as past behavior is one of the best indicators of future evets. While this part of the process can certainly prove tedious, their important cannot be overstated.

After you have determined the historical precedent of the currency pair you are curious about, the next thing you will want to consider is the phase the currency is currently in and how likely it is going to remain in that phase for the foreseeable future. Every currency goes through phases on a regular basis as part of the natural market cycle.

The first phase is known as the boom phase which can be easily identified by its low volatility and high liquidity. The opposite of this phase is known as the bust phase wherein volatility is extremely high, and liquidity is extremely low. There are also pre and post versions of both phases that can be used to determine how much time the phase in question has before it is on its way out. Determining the right phase is a key part of knowing when you are on the right track regarding a particular trading pair.

In order to determine the current major or minor phase, the easiest thing to do is to start by checking the current rates of defaults along with banks loans as well as the accumulated reserve levels of the currencies in question. If numbers are relatively low them a boom phase is likely to be on its way, if not already in full swing. If the current numbers have already overstayed their welcome, then you can be fairly confident that a post-boom phase is likely to start at any time. Alternatively, if the numbers in question are higher than the baseline you have already established then you know that the currency in question is either due for a bust phase or is already experiencing it.

You can make money from either of the major phases as long as you are aware of them early on enough to turn a profit before things start to swing back in the opposite direction. Generally speaking, this means that the faster you can pinpoint what the next phase is going to be, the greater your dividends of any related trades will be.

Broaden your scope: After you have a general idea of the baseline for your favored currencies, as well as their current phases, the next thing you will need to do is look at the state of the global market as a whole to determine how it could possibly affect your trading pair. To ensure this part of the process is as effective as possible you are going to need to look beyond the obvious signs that everyone can see to find the indicators that you know will surely make waves as soon as they make it into the public consciousness.

One of the best places to start looking for this information is in the technology sector as emerging technologies can turn entire economies around in a relatively short period of time.

Technological indicators are often a great way to take advantage of a boom phase by getting in on the ground floor as, once it starts, it is likely to continue for as long as it takes for the technology to be fully integrated into the mainstream. Once it reaches the point of complete saturation then a bust phase is likely going to be on the horizon, and sooner rather than later. If you feel as though the countries responsible for the currencies in question are soon going to be in a post-boom or post-bust phase, then you are going to want to be very careful in any speculative market as the drop-off is sure to be coming and it is difficult to pinpoint exactly when.

If you know that a phase shift is coming, but you aren't quite sure when, then it is a good idea to focus on smaller leverage amounts than during other phases as they are more likely to pay off in the short-term. At the same time, you are also going to want to keep any eye out for long-term positions that are likely to pay out if a phase shift does occur. On the other hand, if the phase you are in currently is just starting out, you can make trades that have a higher potential for risk as the time concerns aren't going to be nearly serious enough to warrant the additional caution.

Look to global currency policy: While regional concerns are often going to be able to provide you with an insight into some long-reaching changes a given currency might experience in the near future, you are also going to want to broaden your search, even more, to include relevant global policies as well. While determining where you are going to start can be difficult at first, all you really need to do is to provide the same level of analysis that you used at the micro level on a macro basis instead. The best place to start with this sort of thing is going to be with the interest rates of the major players including the Federal Reserve, the European Central Bank, the Bank of Japan, the Bank of England and any other banks that may affect the currencies you are considering trading.

You will also need to consider any relevant legal mandates or policy biases that are currently in play to make sure that you aren't blindsided by these sorts of things when the times actually comes to stop doing research and actually make a move. While certainly time consuming, understanding every side of all the major issues will make it far easier to determine if certain currencies are flush with supply where the next emerging markets are likely to appear and what worldwide expectations are when it comes to future interest rate changes as well as market volatility.

Don't forget the past: Those who forget the past are doomed to repeat it and that goes double for forex traders. Once you have a solid grasp on the current events of the day, you are going to want to dig deeper and look for scenarios in the past that match what is currently going on today. This level of understanding will ultimately lead to a greater understanding of the current strength of your respective currencies while also giving you an opportunity to accurately determine the length of the current phase as well.

In order to ensure you are able to capitalize on your knowledge as effectively as possible, the ideal time to jump onto a new trade is going to be when one of the currency pairs is entering a post-boom phase while the other is entering the post-bust phase. This will ensure that the traditional credit channels are not exhausted completely, and you will thus have access to the maximum amount of allowable risk of any market state. This level of risk is going to start dropping as soon as the market conditions hit an ideal state and will continue until the situation with the currencies is reversed so getting in and making a profit when the time is right is crucial to your long-term success.

Don't forget volatility: Keeping the current level of volatility in mind is crucial when it comes to ensuring that the investments you are making are actually going to pay off in a reasonable period of time. Luckily, it is relatively easy to determine the current level of volatility in a given market, all you need to do is to look to that country's stock market. The greater the level of stability the market in question is experiencing, the more confident those who are investing in it are going to remain when means the more stable the forex market is going to remain as well.

Additionally, it is important to keep in mind that, no matter what the current level of volatility may be, the market is never truly stable. As such, the best traders are those who prepare for the worst while at the same time hoping for the best. Generally speaking, the more robust a boom phase is, the lower the overall level of volatility is going to be.

Think outside the box on currency pairs: All of the information that you gather throughout the process should give you a decent idea regarding the current state of the currency pairs you are keeping tabs on. You should now have enough to be able to use this information to determine which pairs are going to be able to provide you with the most potential profit in not just the short-term but the long-term as well. Specifically, you are going to want to keep an eye out for pairs that have complimentary futures so that they will end up with the greatest gap between their two interest rates as possible.

Additionally, you are going to want to consider the gap between countries when it comes to overall output and unemployment rate. When looking into these differences you are also going to need to be aware of the fact that shortages can cause constraints to capacity or when the unemployment rate drops, both of which can lead to inflation as well. This, in turn, leads to an increase in interest rates which leads to a general cooling of the country's economy. As such, these factors are extremely important when it comes to determining the overall disparity between the interest rates of specific countries in the near future.

Furthermore, you are going to want to keep tabs on the amount of debt that the countries in question are dealing with, as well as their reputation of repayment on the global market. Specifically, you are going to want to look for a balanced capital to debt ratio as the healthier that this number is the stronger the national currency is going to be no matter what else is currently taking place. To determine this ratio, you will want to know how much capital each country currently has on hand as well as their position when it comes to other nations and their level of reserves and foreign investment.

Understand their relative trade strength: If you find a currency that is currently in the middle of a boom phase, the overall strength that its fundamentals show will determine how likely those who are holding it in various currency pairs are to hold or sell. The same also goes for currencies that boast an overly strong or overly weak interest rate when compared to other, similar currencies. What this means is that when a given currency is in the earliest part of the boom phase you will be able to easily find a strong market for its related currency pairs which combine agreeable fundamentals and strong interest rates. While all of these factors are important, as a general rule a strong interest rate will always trump subpar fundamentals.

Watch out for market sentiment: While determining specifics in undervalued currencies is useful most of the time, sometimes the market simply doesn't behave in the way that it realistically should. In these cases, it is the market sentiment that has hijacked the price of the currency in question and learning how to stay on the lookout for its influence is guaranteed to save you from some seriously unprofitable trades in the long run.

Like many things in the forex market, this is easier said than done, however, which is why it is best to take the following suggestions related to reading market sentiment to heart if you ever hope to get a clear idea of how strong the momentum regarding a given currency truly is.

Choose the right trend: Each and every move that a currency makes is ultimately based on a trend that started building hours, if not days before. As such, if you spend time trading with either the 15 or 60-minute chart then you may find yourself accidentally moving forward based on part of a larger trend that is ultimately going to end up moving in the opposite direction. As such, in order to avoid such mistakes, you are going to want to start by identifying the trend in the daily chart and then working inward from there until you reach your target chart. This will allow you to more easily determine the breadth of a given chart and allow you to avoid trading based on anterior movement as well.

Find the right price movement: On the topic of price movement, depending on the pair you are trading in, you will likely come across profits that you might not otherwise bank by simply getting a feel for the way your favored currency pairs move on a regular basis. Getting a feel for price movement means understanding the speed at which the pair typically moves, in both directions, to ensure that you know the most effective time to strike.

When the movement is clearly headed in an upwards direction with a quickness, only to slowly descend after the fact, time and again, then you can expect other traders to be steadily buying into the pair without taking the time to do all the relevant research. This, in turn, means you can expect the overall sentiment of the market to be bullish which means you can respond appropriately.

Similar information can also be determined based on the way the market responds when new relevant information, both positive and negative, comes to light. As an example, if there was just a round of positive economic news out of the United Kingdom but the positive change in the GBP and USD pair doesn't seem all that enthusiastic, then you can safely determine that the market is moving in a bearish direction when it comes to GBP/USD.

Watch your indicators of volume: While there are a wide variety of different indicators that measure volume, there are no better means for doing so than the Commitment of Traders Report which is released each and every Friday. This report clearly outlines the net of all the trades made, both long and short, for the week, for both commercial and private traders. This is a great place to start if you aren't sure what currencies to favor as this will show where most of the interest was for the proceeding week.

As previously noted, it is best to always trade on the trend which means that if there are more net longs overall you are going to want to buy and if there are more net shorts overall then you are going to want to sell. When this is not the case is if the buy positions are already at extreme levels then you will want to sell or at least wait until things move in the other direction because there can be no more increase if everyone who is going to buy has already bought. Eventually, you will see a reversal in this case which means that if this is the case then you are better off trading in the medium term instead.

Look more closely at international trends: When you are first getting your start in the forex market you are likely going to be surprised at just how interconnected the world as a whole really is. While some of these connections are going to be obvious, other will certainly catch you off guard the first time you encounter them which means you will want to pay attention to the way news affects various currency pairs, even if you are not actually trading in them at the moment as you never know when that information might be useful again at a later date.

Gdp

Gross Domestic Product of a country is the sum of all the monetary value of all goods and services of a given country within a specific time frame. This monetary value of the goods and services must be produced within the borders of that same country. A country's Gross Domestic Product is calculated annually, although there is a possibility of calculating it quarterly depending on the countries policy concerning the GDP calculation.

Gross Domestic Product is the best economic indicator among other economic indicators. Most people think GDP can never be an indicator because it only measures the market value of the goods and services, but they are wrong. From forex fundamental analysis view, when there is an increase in a gross domestic product without an increase in the demand of the products, this constitutes to a weak economy.

Rate Of Employment

The unemployment rate is another indicator of the health of the economy. High unemployment rates will make the currency unattractive, while lower unemployment rates are going to make the currency more attractive. Again, this is something that has to be seen in a relative context; you are going to compare the unemployment rate to the other partner in the currency pair. You will also want to look at the labor force participation rate if this data is available, as well as the number of people working full-time or part-time.

Inflation Rate

Inflation is the balance between the circulation of money in economic growth and distribution. Each country or market has a set level of which the rise can reach. There is a healthy inflation level and unhealthy inflation level. If the economic growth and money circulation in the market are not maintained, the country or any market is likely to suffer from crippling inflation. The balance between the two brings about a healthy inflation. Every economy works very hard on their economies so that the sound economic level can be maintained.

When inflation is high in any economy, supply and demand are disturbed. Supply gets an advantage because there is more than what is demanded. This high inflation affects the currency negatively. The currency drops. Oppositely, when inflation is low-deflation, there is more demand than supply. During this deflation period, money value rises, and the cost of goods go down in the market. It is a strategy that most economies employ but on a short term basis. If deflation strategy is used long term, it will have adverse effects on the economy. The responsible party will get a hard time stabilizing their economy again.

Balance Of Payments

The "balance of payments" can tell you how healthy the economy is in comparison to others in the world, and it can do so fairly directly. It refers to all international activities and is considered to be in a good state when the country is accepting more payments from other countries than it is making.

BoP, as it is usually written, is the sum of all of the transactions every entity in the country. That sounds like a dizzying amount of data, and it is. It includes all purchases, sales, loans, and debts between all of the people, companies, and banks inside the country as well as the transactions between entities within the country and entities outside of it. An analogy would be if you lived in a house with several roommates, and you all gave each other money to cover various household bills and expenses. Your personal BoP would be all the money you spent on your roommate obligations and all the money you spent out of the house as well.

This is incredibly important to forex traders because it shows the balance between imports and exports in a complete and detailed way. If a country is importing more than it is exporting, its currency will pile up in the market and likely lose value against other currencies. The opposite is true as well. If a country is exporting more than it is importing, more things are being bought with that currency so less of it will be available, strengthening it against other currencies because of increased demand.

Public Debt

An economic indicator is a piece of detailed information about the country financial status. It's released by the government or an organization. The results are released at particular scheduled times that are: weekly, monthly, or even quarterly.

The information released can lead to higher returns in the financial markets. With the data, one can determine whether a countries economy has improved, is stagnant or has decreased. The commotion can occur when prices are released before the release of official rates. This condition is known as "priced market."

When reports are released, traders usually check on the weakness and strength in the various economies before venturing into a trade. The following are economic indicators you should watch out.

Interest Rate

There are different types of interest rates, but the main focus of fundamental forex analysis falls on the nominal and the base interest rates. The central banks of different states set these interest rates. The central bank has to lend money to private banks after creating money. Therefore, the interest amount paid by the private banks on the loans they have acquired from the central bank is called the nominal interest. The nominal interest rate is also known as the base interest rate.

Interest rates balance any economy in the world. It is probably the most reliable economic factor indicator for any forex trader to look at before going into the trade. The interest rates- nominal have a significant influence on the values of the assets, in this case, on the currencies. They also influence other factors like unemployment, manufacturing, investment, and inflation.

Since it is the duty of the central bank control and boost the economy of the country, it makes sure that inflation reaches the country's set level and does not go past that. If it wants to boost the economy of a respective country, it brings down the interest rates. When the nominal interest is down, more private banks will go to the central bank to borrow money while individuals will go to the private banks to borrow money. There will be high production and high consumption correspondently. This act of the central bank will improve the economy of a country but in a short time not a long time.

In as much as interest rates are good at improving the country's economy, it is a poor strategy. The low-interest rates in the markets after a long time will cause over-inflation of cash in the economy and cause an imbalance in this economy. The imbalance caused by this low-interest rates is likely to affect the country for a long time before the economy goes back to normal. Sometimes it paralyzes the country's economy entirely.

However, most of the central banks have a remedy for this inflation. When the economy starts swaying, or after a short period of reducing the interest rates, the central banks increase the scales again. When the interest rates are raised, the money circulating in the market decreases. The private banks will not take loans, and the individuals will not go to the private banks borrow. So when the interest rates start changing, a forex trader should find his opportunity and make an entry or exit in the trade.

A trader should put in mind that the information released on the economic data is critical. He should carefully consider it, with the forex fundamental analysis if he wants to succeed in the forex trade.

Chapter 6. Is Technical Analysis Important in Forex Trading?

Technical analysis is the method of using charts and other recording methods to analyze various data in options trading. Using these visual instruments, you have the chance to determine the direction of the market because they give you a trend.

This method focuses on studying the supply and demand of a market. The price will be seen to rise when the investor realizes the market is undervalued, and this leads to buying. If they think that the market is overvalued, the prices will start falling, and this is deemed the perfect time to sell.

You need to understand the movement of the various indicators to make the perfect decision. This method works on the premise that history usually repeats itself – a huge change in the prices affects the investors in any situation.

History

Technical analysis has been used over the years in trades. The technical analysis methods have been used for over a hundred years to come up with deductions regarding the market.

In Asia, the use of technical analysis led to the development of candlestick techniques, and it forms the main charting techniques.

Over time, more tools and techniques have come up to help traders come up with predictions of the prices in various markets.

There are many indicators that you can use to determine the direction of the market, but only a few are valuable to your course. Let us look at the various indicators and how to use them.

The Benefits Of Technical Analysis In Options Trading

There are a variety of benefits that you enjoy when you use technical analysis in trading options. The benefits arise from the fact that traders are usually asking a lot of questions touching on the price of the market and entry points. While the forecast for prices is a huge task, the use of technical analysis makes it easier to handle.

The major advantages of technical analysis include

Expert Trend Analysis

This is the biggest advantage of technical analysis in any market. With this method, you can predict the direction of the market at any time. You can determine whether the market will move up, down or sideways easily.

Entry and Exit Points

As a trader, you need to know when to place a trade and when to opt out. The entry point is all about knowing the right time to enter the trade for good returns. Exiting a trade is also vital because it allows you to reduce losses.

Leverage Early Signals

Every trader looks for ways to get early signals to assist them in making decisions. Technical analysis gives you signals to trigger a decision on your part. This is usually ideal when you suspect that a trend will reverse soon. Remember the time the trend reverses are when you need to make crucial decisions.

It Is Quick

In options trading, you need to go with techniques that give you fast results. Additionally, getting technical analysis data is cheaper than other techniques in fundamental analysis, with some companies offering free charting programs. If you are in the market to make use of short time intervals such as 1-minute, 5-minute, 30 minute or 1-hour charts, you can get this using technical analysis.

It Gives You a Lot of Information

Technical analysis gives you a lot of information that you can use to make trading decisions. You can easily build a position depending on the information you get then take or exit trades. You have access to information such as chart pattern, trends, support, resistance, market momentum, and other information.

The current price of an asset usually reflects every known information of an asset. While the market might be rife with rumors that the prices might surge or plummet, the current price represents the final point for all information. As the traders and investors change their bearing from one part to another, the changes in asset reflect the current value perception.

If all this turns out to be true, then the only info you require is a price chart that gives all the price reflections and predictions. There isn't any need for you to worry yourself with the reasons why the price is rising or falling when you can use a chart to determine everything.

With the right technical analysis information, you can make trading easier and faster because you make decisions based not on hearsay but facts. You don't have to spend your time reading and trying to make headway in financial news. All you need us to check what the chart tells you.

You Understand Trends

If the prices on the market were to gyrate randomly without any direction, you would find it hard to make money. While these trends run in all directions, the prices always move in trends. Directional bias allows you to leverage the benefits of making money. Technical analysis allows you to determine when a trend occurs and when it doesn't occur, or when it is in reversal.

Many of the profitable techniques that are used by the traders to make money follow trends. This means that you find the right trend and then look for opportunities that allow you to enter the market in the same direction as the trend. This helps you to capitalize on the price movement.

Trends run in various degrees. The degree of the trend determines how much money you make, whether in the short term or long-term trading. Technical analysis gives you all the tools that make it possible for you to do this.

History Always Repeats Itself

Technical analysis uses common patterns to give you the information to trade. However, you need to understand that history will not be exact when it repeats itself, though. The current analysis will be either bigger or smaller, depending on the existing market conditions. The only thing is that it won't be a replica of the prior pattern.

This pans out easily because most human psychology doesn't change so much, and you will see that the emotions have a hand in making sure that prices rise and fall. The emotions that traders exhibit create a lot of patterns that lead to changes in prices all the time. As a trader, you need to identify these patterns and then use them for trading. Use prior history to guide you and then the current price as a trigger of the trade.

Enjoy Proper Timing

Do you know that without proper timing you will not be able to make money at all? One of the major advantages of technical analysis is that you get the chance to time the trades. Using technical analysis, you get to wait, then place your money in other opportunities until it is the right time to place a trade.

Applicable Over a Wide Time Frame

When you learn technical analysis, you get to apply it to many areas in different markets, including options. All the trading in a market is based mostly on the patters that are as a result of human behavior. These patterns can then be mapped out on a chart to be used across the markets.

While there is some difference between analyzing different securities, you will be able to use technical analysis in most of the markets.

Additionally, you can use the analysis in any timeframe, which is applicable whether you use hourly, daily, or weekly charts. These markets are usually taken to be fractal, which essentially means that patterns that appear on a small scale will also be present on a large scale as well.

Technical Analysis Secrets To Become The Best Trader

To make use of technical analysis the right way, you need to follow time-testing approaches that have made the technique a gold mine for many traders. Let us look at the various tips that will take you from novice to pro in just a few days:

Use More than One Indicator

Numbers make trading easy, but it also applies to the way you apply your techniques. For one, you need to know that just because one technical indicator is better than using one, applying a second indicator is better than using just one. The use of more than one indicator is one of the best ways to confirm a trend. It also increases the odds of being right.

As a trader, you will never be 100 percent right at all times, and you might even find that the odds are stashed against you when everything is plain to see. However, don't demand too much from your indicators such that you end up with analysis paralysis.

To achieve this, make use of indicators that complement each other rather than the ones that clash against each other.

Go for Multiple Time Frames

Using the same buy signal every day allows you to have confidence that the indicator is giving you all you need to know to trade. However, make sure you look for a way to use multiple timeframes to confirm a trend. When you have a doubt, it is wise that you increase the timeframe from an hour to a day or from a daily chart to a weekly chart.

Understand that No Indicator Measures Everything

You need to know that indicators are supposed to show how strong a trend is; they won't tell you much more. So, you need to understand and focus on what the indicator is supposed to communicate instead of working with assumptions.

Go with the Trend

If you notice that an option is trading upward, then go ahead and buy it. Conversely when the trend stops trending, then it is time to sell it. If you aren't sure of what is going on in the market at that time, then don't make a move.

However, waiting might make you lose profitable trades as opposed to trading. You also miss out on opportunities to create more capital.

Have the Right Skills

It really takes superior analytical capabilities and real skill to be successful at trading, just like any other endeavor. Many people think that it is hard to make money with options trading, but with the right approach, you can make extraordinary profits.

You need to learn and understand the various skills so that you know what the market seeks from you and how to achieve your goals.

Trade with a Purpose

Many traders go into options trading with the main aim of having a hobby. Well, this way you won't be able to make any money at all. What you need to do is to trade for the money – strive to make profits unlike those who try to make money as a hobby.

Always Opt for High value

Well, no one tells you to trade any security that comes your way – it is purely a matter of choice. Try and go for high-value options so that you can trade them the right way. Make use of fundamental analysis to choose the best options to trade in.

Be Disciplined

When using technical analysis, you might find yourself in situations that require you to make a decision fast. To achieve success, you need to have strict risk management protocols. Don't base on your track record to come up with choices; instead, make sure you follow what the analysis tells you.

Don't Overlook Your Trading Plan

The trading plan is in place to guide you when things go awry. Coming up with the plan is easy, but many people find it hard to implement the plan the right way. The trading plan has various components – the signals and the take-profit/stop-loss rules. Once you get into the market, you need to control yourself because you have already taken a leap. Remember you cannot control the indicators once they start running – all you can do is to prevent yourself from messing up everything.

Come up with the trading rules when you are unemotional to try and mitigate the effects of making bad decisions.

Accept Losses

Many people trade with one thing in mind – losses aren't part of their plan. This is a huge mistake because you need to understand that every trade has two sides to it – a loss and a profit. Remember that the biggest mistake that leads to losses isn't anything to do with bad indicators rather using them the wrong way. Always have a stop-loss order when you trade to prevent loss of money.

Have a Target When You Trade

So, what do you plan to achieve today? Remember, trading is a way to grow your capital as opposed to saving. Options trading is a business that has probable outcomes that you get to estimate. When you make a profit, make sure you take some money from the table and then put it in a safe place.

Importance Of A Technical Analysis

There are many uncertainties in this market. But as a trader, you have to take a risk and work on probabilities. As much as the market can be chaotic, you will identify patterns and make the most out of it. With a clear review of the charts, and study of the market, you have the potential of making the correct choices when it comes to your trade. You will know when to enter a market. And, the most important thing is, you learn how to get out of a trade and when.

Secondly, you learn to identify patterns mark can figure out what to do when particular issues arise in the market.

Also, you get to learn to determine the probabilities and jump into the right opportunities, when odds work on your favor.

How Do You Conduct a Technical Analysis?

- Determine which security interests you -For instance, you can do research on which sector is at the moment trading this will assist in deciding on what to buy or sell

- Choose a strategy that suits you -each stock is unique. And each cannot utilize the same approach.
- Choose a trading account. To maximize profits, go for the account with the right functionality, cost, and also support.
- Comprehend your tools -Knowing thee tools that fit your trading strategies and tools is essential. Free tools are available for you to learn and understand the features.
- Try out to test your system with the market data before jumping on the bandwagon of trading. Choose a few indicators that can fit the technical indicator requirements you chose. Monitor how they perform each day.

Advantages of Technical Analysis

You learn when to exist and enter a trade- through the patterns in charts; you will learn how to jump out of a trade.

They provide you with the right information directions are essential to in any field. Technical analysis offers precisely what you need to navigate this industry.

Get information on the current trends- prices tend to increase or decrease. Usually, they reflect on the information of an existing asset to make decisions.

Differences between fundamental and technical analysis

As much as the two analysis help you get trading results. They have numerous differences. Some are here below

Fundamental analysis uses economic reports of industry statistics and news events to analyze data and make predictions; also, it forecasts share prices on the basis company statics and economic industry. Technical analysis uses a chart to analyze data and majorly focuses on internal data and market statistics.

Fundamental analysis is concerned with the investments. The investors usually hold or buy a stock of a company with the information they got. Technical analysis is more concerned with the trade.

The security of the future prices is determined by the past and present performance a company makes, in Forex trading, while indicators and charts are the ones that determine the future market prices .

A long-term trader usually utilizes fundament analysis. Long term investors buy stocks containing enormous dividends pay-out and regularly release or sell them after several years when the stocks have passed through several fluctuations while short berm traders usually utilize technical analysis.

Such traders did not buy or keep goods for years, but instead, they focus more on short term profits.

Fundamental utilizes the intrinsic value of stock got when one analyses income statements like cash flow management, profit margins, and returns on equity. They predict the future of the market. A technical analysis, depends on charts, technical indicators, resistance, and support to analyze future trend patterns.

In fundamental analysis, no assumptions are made while assumptions like similar price trends are not news, in technical analysis.

Fundamentals analysts don't need to go back to history to find to discover past prices and the fluctuations incurred. However, technicians trade re-occurs, and the possibility of history repeating itself is high.

So which analysis techniques should you choose?

Most analysis on street walls prefers fundamental analysis to technical analysis. Both technical and fundamental have their advantages and disadvantages. But a good investor will point out that their combination of both the two, end up producing t exceptional results.

Risk management

Knowledge of both fundamental and technical approach can help to handle any risk involved in a trade. Economic can tell if the attitude of particular market changes, but fails to inform you when the view of the market is wrong. Technical analysis helps you manage risk as you can view on the charts and can help you revise a market view.

Also, a combination of the two analyses can confirm specific trends. When, most people in a country expect a higher interest rate, but it doesn't manifest, then that countries' currency would likely decrease in value. Furthermore, When the currency continues rising, there could be a possibility of other factors involved rather than the interest rate. A technical trader can use the way markets reacts to fundamental news to their advantage.

Support And Resistance

As an instrument moves, either in a direction or sideways, as a result of the underlying order flow, it encounters certain areas on the chart where it experiences a change in the character of the order flow and this is reflected as a reaction on the price chart. These areas can be called support or resistance or S/R for short.

S/R areas are places where the players in the market agree upon something and this is what causes the price to ricochet off the levels in a particular direction. Most newbie traders make the mistake of thinking of S/R as straight lines on a chart. Another common mistake or source of confusion is determining which S/R level matters. It is quite common to see a bunch of lines on a chart marking all the S/R levels. The key to these questions is, as always, order flow.

Order Flow and S/R

You're probably getting sick of the term order flow by now. However, it is essential that you drill this into your head that there is nothing more important to your trading than understanding order flow. Everything that traders do, be it using indicators or algorithms is geared towards understanding this, above all else.

Let's say an imbalanced order flow produces a strong trend and price bursts in the direction of the dominant order flow. As price progresses, there eventually comes a point where the counter-trend players think, "this has gone on long enough" and push back. In the initial stages, this challenge isn't very successful and price moves on. Eventually, though, the counter-trend players are successful in halting the trend charge and produce a significant reaction.

The level at which this reaction occurs becomes significant now. This is where, for the first time, the counter-trend players took a stand and said "enough!" and managed to push back significantly into the trend. As a result of this, the counter-trend traders who were hesitant to take part in the market, read this level as being a place where they will surely have the support of other counter-trend players.

The with trend traders, meanwhile, also take note of this level and realize that given the larger number of counter-trend orders present at that level, they need greater force to push through it.

This level then becomes a line of sorts where the buyers and sellers do battle and no matter the result, the chart landscape ends up bearing the marks of this battle. You may think of it as battle lines being drawn.

This, in short, is what an S/R level is. This is also why levels are very rarely straight, horizontal lines and are instead zones. The market is a chaotic place and it is unreasonable to expect order at all times, especially when you have both sides of the market colliding with considerable force and intention to prevail.

Key and Non-Key S/R

Not every battle line is significant. Much like how in real battles, certain areas are of greater strategic value than others, some levels pose greater significance than others. There are some pretty simple keys to determining whether a level is key or not. First off, the number of times price has touched the level in the past and bounced off it is the clearest indication of a key level.

The second indication you can use to determine a key level is to see whether it is significant on a higher time frame. As beginner traders, you don't have to worry yet about trading multiple time frames. You simply look at the time frame above the one you are currently on and see whether the level is present on there as well.

From an order flow perspective, let's look at why these two characteristics indicate key S/R zones. Price repeatedly bouncing off a level indicates the presence of a significant number of traders at the level who are invested in protecting that level and not letting it be breached. The fact that this occurs over time, repeatedly, is of even greater significance because it effectively means even time cannot dampen their enthusiasm for defending that level. This, in turn, gives confidence to other traders who didn't take part previously but can see that this time, they can count on the support of other traders and hence, take part in defending the level.

As for the second indication, where levels are present on higher time frames, this tells us that not only are traders on the current time frame defending this level, but traders on a higher time frame with completely different holding times and strategies are invested in defending the level too. Given the diverse nature of traders holding the level, it makes sense that breaching it will require a lot of force and this will, therefore, be a key battle zone.

Order Flow Determines Key Levels

Following from this, we can see how the underlying order flow characteristics make levels key or non-key. We can extend this conclusion in a few ways further. The strength of a level (in other words how key it is) is dependent on the order flow currently present in the chart landscape.

Think of it this way. You're driving a car at 100 MPH on a highway and you happen to come across a wall of bricks, 1 brick wide, and which is the same height as the hood of your car. Let's assume you don't have time to hit the brake even a little, and hit this wall. Quite unpleasant, of course. However, your car will almost certainly plow through the wall and destroy it. Your car will suffer extensive damage of course but the wall will be non-existent.

Now let's say, instead of a car, you're flying the USS Enterprise at warp speed towards this wall and strike it. Not only will this wall be obliterated but your starship will suffer nothing more than a dent or some chipped paint. The wall doesn't really pose much of a challenge to you then.

If you strike this same wall in your car at a speed of 10 MPH though, the wall will almost certainly prevail. Your car may not suffer much damage but that is beside the point. The wall will hold and if your objective is to break through the wall, you will need much greater force. The threat that the wall poses to you is not determined just by how strong that wall is but by how much stronger your force applied to it is.

This is pretty much what happens when price approaches any level on the chart. The greater the order flow imbalance behind the move, the less of a challenge that level poses (in terms of holding up the trend). The greater the balance behind a move, the more of a challenge and thus significant, a level is. This is how order flow helps us determine what a key S/R level is as opposed to one that isn't.

Most traders, without taking order flow into account, simply look at just the strength of the level. Going back to our example, if you were on the starship Enterprise at warp speed and encountered a tiny (relatively speaking) brick wall, would you come to screeching halt and call for backup to deal with this "threat" in your way? Sounds absurd, doesn't it? Yet this is what traders do when they only look at the level without taking into account the order flow characteristics.

Different S/R for Different Environments

It follows from the above that the levels you need to pay attention to are different depending upon the environment in which price is in, or, the nature of the order flow. If we're at the beginning of a trend, which sees huge with trend participation, the brick wall that can conceivably stop this force needs to be quite large. Thus, you do not need to be worried about a minor level that price is approaching, with the trend, in such an environment.

Now it is important to identify levels that will push the price with the trend and against the trend. In a strongly trending, imbalanced environment, you shouldn't worry about the trend being reversed at minor levels. However, you will need to consider such levels as key levels to enter with the trend.

Reading the characteristics of order flow in a detailed manner is a more advanced skill but well worth mastering. Once you're fluent in it, you won't need any other indicator to trade anything.

All you'll need is a price chart. For now, though, keep the below checklist in mind to get a feel for the order flow:

- How steep is the trend? The steeper it is, the greater the number of with trend traders.
- What is the level of counter-trend participation? Are counter-trend traders able to push the price back into the trend? How long are they able to keep the trend from continuing?
- What is the color distribution of bars in the current trend? Is it an even mix? Is one color steadily increasing? Decreasing?

The answers to the above 3 points will give you a good idea of what the bull/bear distribution is.

Chapter 7. Resistance and Dynamic Supports

You will most likely already know that the supports and resistances are points on the graph whose price has changed direction in the past. Several times the price rebounds in one place and the stronger the support or resistance that is created. The most important thing to remember when we are going to trade this instrument is that in a trending market after resistance is overcome it becomes support (and vice versa).

Candlesticks

The candlestick has three parts. The first part is the rectangular area that is found in the center of the candlestick. This is called the body. The body of the candlestick tells you the opening and closing prices of the trading session. However, there are two types of candlesticks. Traditionally they are black and white, but I am going to skip over that because who uses black and white charts anymore. I can assure you that almost nobody does.

The background of most charts these days is either black or white. We are going to take the latter possibility, first because most Forex traders actually use black background charts. But you can use white backgrounds and some traders too.

There are two types of candlesticks. A candlestick can indicate that the price dropped for the trading period, in which case it is called a "bearish" candlestick. Or the candlestick can indicate that the price increased over the trading period, in which case it's a bullish candlestick.

On a chart with a white background, a bearish candlestick is red in color. A bullish candlestick will be green in color. On a black chart, the bearish candlesticks are usually solid white, and the bullish candlesticks are the green outline.

That is all pretty basic to understand. Now let us use a basic fact to explain the price action described or illustrated by a candlestick. If there is a bearish trading session, that means that the opening price was higher than the closing price. As a result, the top of the candlestick body – which is a higher pricing point – represents the opening price for the trading session. In contrast, the bottom of the candlestick, which is the lower price on the chart, represents the closing price for the trading session.

A bullish candlestick works in the opposite way. A bullish candlestick indicates that the price went up during the trading session. So the top of the candlestick is the closing price for the trading session. The bottom of the candlestick is going to be the opening price for the trading session.

A candlestick has lines that come out of the top and bottom of the body. These lines are called shadows or wicks. They have the same meaning whether or not the candlestick is bullish, or whether it's bearish. The wick or shadow coming out of the top of the candlestick body tells you the high price of the trading session. The bottom wick tells you the low price of the trading session. The basics of candlestick setup are shown below.

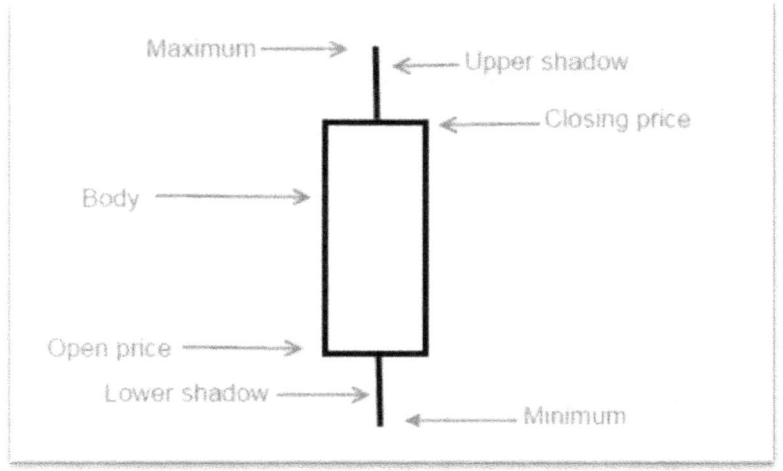

Pin Bar Pattern

The pin bar pattern is our main signal to enter the market, the most effective and accurate. It's one of the most effective and profitable patterns I've ever seen and it has helped me earn a lot of money. The pin bar is characterized by a very small body that is located at one end and a long shadow (or shadow). This candle indicates that there is a strong ongoing variation in terms of trends and, located in strong supports or resistances in favor of trends, it has a success rate of over 80%. It also allows you to easily position the Stop Loss (SL), this always to correct Money Management and risk management. Later in the book, we will also see where to place Stop Loss and Take Profit respectively by following our main rules:

- Trend is your friend

- Let profits run and cut losses

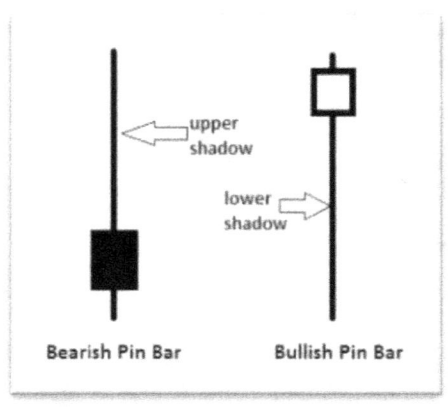

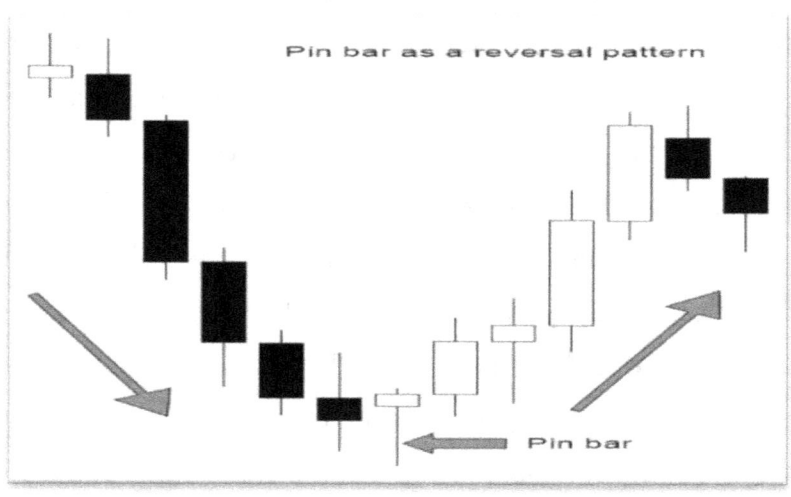

Engulfing Pattern

The Engulfing pattern is another very strong price formation that we are going to trade. It is a slightly less effective formation than the pin bar but, if positioned on strong supports or resistances, it guarantees a success rate of over 70%. We will call it Bullish Engulfing when it is a bullish signal and Bearish Engulfing when the signal is bearish. Here are some examples of the Engulfing pattern.

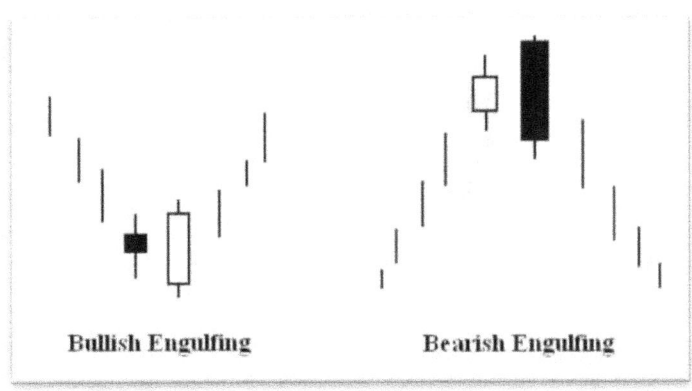

Morning Star / Evening Star

Another strong signal of price reversal if located in areas of strong support or resistance. Of the signs we will use in strategy, this is the least effective. It has a success rate of around 60%. It is characterized by a strong directional candle immediately followed by a small indecision candle (often a Doji, or a candle without a body or with a very small body), followed by a strong candle in the opposite direction. If the central or indecisive candle that is formed is a Pin Bar, the signal is much more powerful.

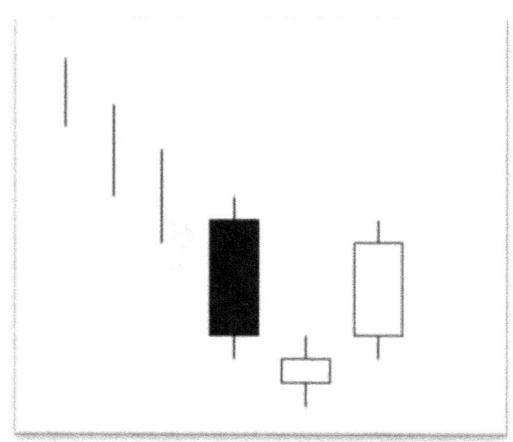

Operational Risk Reward

The operations will be set only in favor of trends (remember? Trend is your friend) and the average Risk Reward is approximately 1 to 3. This means that for every 10 Euros with which we go to operate, it can generate 30 Euros profit. This RR will allow us to be profitable even by doing just 3 out of 10 operations. Example. Total transactions 10 Success rate 30% Loss transactions 7 - Total loss 70 Profit operations 3 - Total profit 90 Net profit = 20 Earning with only 30% of profit operations is priceless. Personally, I have a success rate of about 60% of the total operations, this guarantees me a very high margin.

Stop Loss And Take Profit

Now let's see where to place Stop Loss and Take Profit respectively of our operations for each pattern and in every situation. Usually, the Stop Loss is placed at the end of the candle that starts the trade. The Take Profit instead is placed in the first resistance or support opposite the candle.

Money Management

MM money management or capital management is an essential component to not burn your Trading account. How many times have you seen people who made big money and then lost everything in a single wrong transaction? Here is what we want to avoid. On many blogs or trading sites, it is recommended to use 2% of the capital for each trade. This means that if the operation fails, only 2% is lost. In our case, each profit operation would generate a profit of around 5-6%. This percentage approach is a bit obsolete, in fact, in my opinion, you should not rely on fixed percentages but the MM should take into account the maximum loss capacity of a person. How much are you willing to lose for each operation in such a way that the operations you are going to do remain purely mechanical and that they do not affect your emotions? For example, with a capital of 10'000 euros there would be and a standard 2% approach you would have to risk 200 euros for each operation. 200 euros are right for you? If your legs are trembling just at the thought of losing 200 euros then most likely you will have to enter operation with a smaller amount. Maximum comfort in operating is essential to become a successful trader. Anyone who gets caught up in emotion and does not follow MM's rules will soon reset his capital to zero. And always remember that it is enough for us to do just 30% of the operations to earn.

Reversal Signals

Now we need to be able to look for certain signals that indicate a coming change in price trend. The signals are in the price action that tells us that traders are adopting a different sentiment, and the price is about to change direction. This is something you can spend a great deal of time educating yourself about. However, there is only a small subset of indicators that you need to be aware of.

Drawing Trend Lines

Drawing trend lines is a simple method that can be used to determine where pricing is going to end up, if the market appears to be moving strongly in one direction or the other. No matter which direction the price is moving, there are always going to be fluctuations. So let's consider a downward trend first. A part of the fluctuation is the fact that on the way down, there are always going to be peaks that occur, that is the asset will drop in price, then rise back up for a short time, then drop in price again, and repeat the process, with each peak as it rises up again getting smaller and smaller. This natural feature of declining prices makes it easy to estimate trends. Starting at the top peak, draw a straight line from the top of the peak, passing the line through all the peaks on the way downward. You want to extend the line past the current price so that you can get an estimate of future price levels, if the market continues to decline. This will be a downward sloping line.

If you are looking at an upward trend instead, you start at the first dip or trough in price. Then draw a straight line, with an upward slope, that connects the bottoms of all the dips on the way up to the right of the chart. This will allow you to get an estimate of where the price is heading if the trend continues.

Most trading platforms allow you to draw trend lines right on their charts on the screen, so you don't actually have to print out a chart and do this on a piece of paper, to estimate where the price is going. You will simply have to position the line in the right locations.

Simple Moving Averages

One of the most popular of the other types of moving averages is called an exponential moving average. This moving average tends to give more accurate information. The reason that it's able to do so is that the exponential moving average weights the prices. The mathematical details aren't important for traders to know, you only have to note that when you use an exponential moving average, prices that are closer to the current trading period are given higher weights than long ago prices. This means that an exponential moving average curve is going to emphasize recent prices, as opposed to long ago prices.

The use of moving averages is so common that trading platforms, like metatrader, are going to show them below your pricing chart by default. An example is shown below, with crossover points indicated by the white arrows.

The way to do your analysis is to combine what you see with the candlesticks with what the moving averages are telling you. In my experience, the moving averages tend to be very accurate indicators of upcoming trends. However, it remains to be seen if the trend reversal is strong or long-lasting.

You can use a two-step process. The first step is to closely follow the candlestick patterns to look for indicators that a reversal is coming. If you see that the candlesticks are showing signs of a trend reversal, then you can check the moving averages to confirm or deny. If they confirm what you see on the candlestick charts, then you can make a move on a position, whether it is opening a new position or closing an existing position. So you can eyeball them with the candlesticks in real-time.

It can be good to practice with this before actually entering trades and putting real money at risk. Just spend a few days closely watching a currency pair, and begin to identify the patterns seen in the candlesticks in real-time.

Another chart option that you can look at is called the relative strength index or RSI. This can be used in conjunction with your other tools. The purpose of this indicator is to tell you if there are "overbought" or "oversold" conditions. Overbought means that there has been too much buying and that the price is higher than it should be. When there are overbought conditions, chances are there is going to be a trend reversal.

Oversold is the opposite situation; there has been too much selling off of the asset. In the case of oversold conditions, too many people sold the asset off, and as a result, prices have gone down to levels that are lower than conditions really justify.

The value of the RSI will tell you if conditions are neutral, overbought, or oversold. If conditions are neutral, the RSI will be ranging between 20 and 80. If conditions are overbought, this is demonstrated by an RSI that is higher than 80. Finally, if conditions are oversold, this is demonstrated by an RSI that is lower than 20. These values are not fixed, however. Some traders who are more conservative use a narrower range, such as 30-70.

Just like other indicators, you should not use the RSI in isolation, or take action based solely on what the RSI is telling you. Let's take the case of a rising price trend. If the RSI is telling you that the asset is overbought, you see a crossing of the short-term moving average below the long-term moving average, and the candlesticks are indicating a trend reversal, this is a strong selling signal.

Now consider in a downtrend. If the RSI falls below 20 indicating that the asset is oversold, and you see the short-term moving average crossing above the long-term moving average, with signals of a trend reversal coming from the candlesticks, then you have evidence that is strong enough to take as a buying signal. So you can see that we will take multiple signals together, to confirm what we see in the candlesticks. If the candlestick patterns are not confirmed, then you might want to hold off on making a buying decision.

Patience Is The Key

If you decide to use this strategy, you must know in advance that it is very profitable but requires a lot of patience to be carried out. Forget about doing 3 or 5 or 10 trades a day, forget about compulsive trading. 1 or 2 trades per month will be enough to obtain even 10% monthly returns, all of this with only 10 minutes a day. Remember that we are looking for freedom and not a job, so this system has been designed to obtain the results of a professional trader but staying in front of the screen as little time as possible so that we can use our time to do what most like it. Do not force operations in any way, if the rules are not respected in detail, do not enter the market and simply wade. Wait for the perfect pattern and situation and the markets will be your ATM. Respect the system I taught you and the results will come by itself. Ps. Start learning and practicing with a demo account. When you have full mastery of the strategy you can switch to a Real account with incredible results.

Chapter 8. Practical Trading Strategies

There are many different ways that people run their businesses ranging from the traditional means to more sophisticated means.

The most important aspect in every successful business however, and more especially in Forex trading, is the selection of the most assorted strategies to be applied in different conditions.

Those who have followed entirely one system of trade have found out that it won't offer solutions to the ever changing technology and complexity of the market demands for Forex trade.

It is important for every single trader to have the knowledge and skills of challenging the market circumstances of which is not very easy. It demands for a deep knowledge and revelation of the economics.

In this topic we are going to provide you with the necessary but simple strategies that if applied can lead to a successful Forex business. Recall: these strategies are friendly for the novice traders who would wish to step up their knowledge and skills.

There are various ways in which these trading strategies can be classified. We will consider the basic classifications.

Analysis-Based Trading Strategies
Technical Analysis

As the names suggests, 'analysis', this method focuses primarily on the evaluation of the market trends through charts as a means of predicting the to-be price trends of the market.

In this method, an evaluation of assets is done basing on statistics and past analysis of market actions like the then volumes and the past prices.

Technical analysis is not done with a primary objective of weighing the underlying value of assets; instead, charts with other measuring tools are used to define the patterns that are helpful in future forecast in market actions.

It is believed that the market's future performance is easily determined by the past trends in its performance.

Trend Trading

In technical analysis, a trend is a very critical aspect. The tools used in this type of analysis, have a common motive which is simply to determine trends of the market. Therefore, to trend is to move; in this context it means the way the market is moving.

As we know, fore market is a wavy and zigzag motion that represents the successive trails that define clearly troughs and peaks which are sometimes called lows and highs'?

Depending on the available trends of the lows and highs, it is possible for a trader to define the nature of the market type.

Other than the popular notion of the highs and lows, there is yet another format of the trends in Forex trading called: uptrend/downtrend and sideways trend.

Support and Resistance

It is quite imperative to know the meaning of the horizontal level before defining the support and resistance strategy. This is the level in the price signifying market support of resistance. In technical analysis, resistance and support as used refer to the lows or highs in prices in that order.

Support in this case refers to an area on a chart which shows that the interest in buying is stronger than the selling force.

This is revealed though successive troughs. On the other hand, resistance level, as represented on the chart refers to an area where the buying force is outweighed by the selling concern.

Range Trading

It is also referred to as channel trading. This signifies the absence market direction that may be associated with lack of trends. It is used to identify the movement in the prices of currencies within the channels of which it is tasked to establish the range in the movements.

It can be achieved by linking sets of lows and highs to the horizontal-trend line. This is to say that the trader is tasked to establish the resistance and support levels with the area in the midst which we refer to as trading-range.

Technical Indicators

When we talk of the technical indicators in reference to Forex trade, we simply refer to the calculations that are inclined to the volume and the price of a given security.

When used, they are meant to corroborate quality and trend in the chart patterns as well enable traders to identify sell and buy signals altogether. These indicators in technical analysis can create sell and buy signals via divergence as well as crossovers.

Whenever the prices go across the moving-average, crossovers are seen however, divergence occurs only if the indicator and the price trends both move in different and opposite directions implying that there is a weakening in the price-trend.

Forex Charts

In Technical analysis, we refer to a chart as a representation of the shifts in prices within a given time frame graphically. It reveals the movement in the security price over a period of time.

Different charts can be applied in search of diversified information and the skills and knowledge of the researcher. There are several types of charts available for your review such as: point and figure, candlestick, line-chart as well as bar charts.

Forex volume

Forex volume indicates the total lots by number, traded in a certain time interval. The higher the volume, the higher the level of pressure; this is as indicated by chart specialists.

They can easily define the downward or the upward shifts in volume by observing the volume bars on the lower side of the charts. When a price movement is accompanied with a high volume, it becomes more valuable than if it is accompanied by low volumes.

Multiple Time-Frame Analysis

Lot price must be tracked over a period (turnover) and in a unique time frame. This is so because a lot price will tend to go through a series or time frames and therefore analysts need to review several time frames so that they establish the lot's trade cycle.

Trading-Style Based Strategies

This is yet another technique which offers a different way of classifying the trading styles. Through trading styles, trading strategies can be created which could include but not limited to buy-and-hold strategy, portfolio trading, trading algorithm, order and carry trades,

It is entirely dependent on your level of understanding, power and your weaknesses that determines the strategies that you will apply. Everyone needs a trading strategy which best suits his desires according to his ability to apply it.

There is no single ever trading style that one must apply whenever he wants to trade because, what suits one person may not suit you and your needs.

Day Trading

This is the act holding a position as well as disposing it off the very same day. This implies that, this type of person does not hold as security for more than a day. There are several strategies that are applied in day trading: fading, momentum, scalping as well as pivot trading.

You have the right if only you have the ability of conducting more than one type of trade in a single day as long as you do not hold a position for more than one day. This means than before the closure of the market, you must have liquidated all your open positions.

There is a challenge in this day trading in that, if you cling on a position for so long, the chances of losing it go high. Based on whatever style you are using, the targets in the price may vary.

Scalping Strategy

This is characterized by short and quick operations and is applied mainly to achieve vast returns on small price variations. Scalpers are able to initiate over 200 trades per day with an intention of making good profits on small shifts in price levels.

Fading strategy

Fading in this case refers to a trade that is initiated against trends. When the trend shifts upwards, faders do sell hoping that there will be a price drop-down; similarly, they may buy as the prices go up.

They buy when the price is escalating and sell when the prices are coming down a notion called fading. It is very contrary to other trends and also to nature of business.

The trade is usually against the usual trends with reasons such as: the buyers at hand may be risking, the currency lots are usually over purchased as well as the earlier may be set for profits.

Daily-Pivot Trading

Currencies are very volatile and as such, traders may wish to capitalize on that to make profits. This is exactly the case with pivot strategy.

A turning point same as the pivot point is a very critical yet unique pointer obtained through the computation of the statistical average of the low, high as well as closing-prices of currency-pairs.

The secret to this strategy lies in the aspect of purchasing currencies at their lowest prices and selling them of at their best prices in the course of the day.

Mathematically it could be represented as follows: [pivot point= (previous close + previous low + previous high)/3]

Momentum Strategy

This is characterized by defining the strongest position that will end up trading highest. In this case, the trader may drop the currency with signs of dropping in price and go for that currency that has positive signs of going up through the day.

A momentum trader has got several indicators which help him detect the trends in the currency lots before he makes his decisions called momentum-oscillators. Such a trader will tend to invest deeply to news feeds which he entirely depends on for price predetermination and decision making.

Buy & Hold Strategy

In this case, a position is bought and held for quite long before being sold so that the prices escalate even if it takes long. Whoever does this has no business with the short term price changes as well as indications. However, this type of strategy best suits the stock traders.

In this case, technical analysis becomes invalid because the trader here is a passive investor who has no rush in determining the market trends of the stocks and currency lots.

Order-Types Trading Strategies

Trading on order will help the trader to join or move out of a position at the very right time by use of various orders which include but not limited to market, pending limit, stop-loss, and stop as well as other orders

At this particular moment, most advanced platforms are fitted with different kinds of orders for trading that are not the common buy/sell buttons. Every order type signifies a certain strategy. You must have the knowledge of how and perhaps when to handle orders before you can use them effectively.

The following are trader orders that can be applied by traders.

- Market order- is put to enable the trader to buy/sell at the ripe price.
- Pending order-enable traders to buy/sell at previously set prices.

- Limit order-guides the trader to buy/sell assets at specific price levels.
- Stop-loss order-is placed to lower a trade risk.

Algorithmic Based Strategy

This is as well referred to as 'automated' Forex trade. There is software designed to help in predetermination of times for purchasing and selling of the securities. This software operates on signals drawn from the technical analysis.

To trade with this type of strategy, you need to issue instructions over the kind of signals that you would wish to search for and its subsequent interpretation. This is an example of a high trading platform which comes with other supportive platforms for trading.

However, Net-TradeX is a platform for trading whereby other than its normal functionalities, presents automated-trading through its advisors.

This is referred to as secondary-platform that yields automatic trading and further sophisticates its processes through a language called: "Net-TradeX language."

It goes ahead to provide room for some trading operations traditionally for example; to open and to close a position to place orders as well as use of the technical tools for analysis purposes.

Meta-Trader 4 similarly is a trading platform which makes it possible to use and execute algorithmic trade via an incorporated program-language "MQL4". It is in this type of platform where traders can come up with called-Advisors, trading–robots with indicators of their own. All acts of making advisors which include: to debug, to test, to optimize and to compile the program are all done and made active through the meta-Trader 4 editor.

Robots are made in this case to take away the emotional concept of the traders which in most cases hinders the free and competent engagement in the trade across the platforms. Emotions have and supply negative attitude to the traders especially when there is a hope for a loss.

Chapter 9.   Winning Psychology for Trading

With a correct attitude towards forex trading, you can be sure to achieve your goals. Here are a few suggestions that can help you develop the correct attitude and mindset for forex trading and trading in general.

Be Patient

This is a virtue when it comes to forex trading as it helps one cover everything at the right time and with the right state of mind. Patience can get you out of trouble as sometimes you might be forced to enter into a market hastily without understanding how it works. For beginners, patience is the key aspect as you get to understand the pros and cons of forex trading. Patience also keeps you away from reacting out of a bad day in business and even making wrong choices and decisions that can cause big losses. As the adage goes, Patience pays, so take your time off a hectic day and trust the process.

Be Objective

In forex trading, one is required to be objective and not trade with emotions. As stated earlier, a forex trader should keep the eyes on the final product, that is, his financial goals. Being subjective or acting on emotions is disastrous for any business and learning to act by the book is key to a successful forex trading career. This means that you should not also listen to people who claim to be Pros in the game and trust your trading patterns instead of sheepishly following the crowd. This doesn't however mean that you should not trade on mass thinking but if you do, always keep in mind that the masses are not always right.

Be Disciplined

This ought to be a major aspect in every business and as earlier pointed out, discipline keeps one out of overreacting for a loss or a win. This cuts across happy and sad moments in business as both sides can affect the outcome if not subjected to some discipline. Being able to control yourself, to not overtrade or under trade and take just enough risks is a skill that can be learned by following procedures and sticking to the game-plan. Remember, you should never, ever, stake half your capital, risk all your profits or worse, trade with money you don't have or money you can't afford to lose.

Be Realistic

Just like any other business, one should be real and expect a particular profit according to the capital traded-in. Always remember that forex trading is not like Lotto or betting where one can win a jackpot of a million dollars by stalking just a little money. It takes time to build up your skills, your knowledge and your confidence and secure good profits with forex trading. Therefore, one should expect the right amount of returns on investment and what comes with it. By not giving up, being disciplined and patient, and doing your research, you might end up achieving your goals and reaching top-level in the forex world. This mentality also helps one to limit the number and types of transactions or operations on a daily or weekly basis and to stay in the game even after losing a small percentage of the initial investment. This is a business opportunity just like any other.

With all said and done, there are rules to abide by in order to reach your potential and most importantly realize your potential in terms of profit. Below are 12 rules that can help you achieve your goals in forex Trading.

1 Trust The Process

Forex trading is a business and needs time and effort to grow and consolidate which means that there is more than just waiting for profits. Profit oriented businesses can end badly if the thresholds one has set are not met and the overall approach is not thoroughly planned. Any business is not only buying and selling as it involves huddles and logistics to make the whole institution work and doable. Some profit oriented forex traders tend to give up easily if they don't meet their target after a few operations or a short period of time. However, one can set a timeline and work towards meeting the set target without having to achieve a specific point which might turn to be the opposite. To achieve your goals, some points are process-oriented and help in reaching the high note in forex trading and are outlined.

2 Outline Daily Activities

Day to day activities can only be achieved when put down on paper for a specific task in forex trading. Having in mind the right thing to do on a specific day is good as it helps avoiding distractions and other things that may get in the way on a business day. This means that the more you know what you are doing on a busy day, you will not waste time doing other things that do not help achieve your goal and the needs you want to build your forex trading skills.

3 Analyze The Market

As pointed out earlier, trading with emotions is bad for business as it does not go by the plans and strategy but with the reaction of business gone wrong or even a big win. Being greedy is so bad in forex trading and it is advisable to analyze the market first before trying out forex trading and giving a shot on the most promising patterns. When you play by the rules, you train the mind to follow the right procedures and even helps in becoming more discipline in forex trading. Training the mind helps in a vulnerable situation which will make you hold on when there is a crisis.

4 Be Defensive

This is another important rule to follow in forex trading for it is the core purpose of joining the business and what will keep you survive storms that will come your way in one way or the other. This simply means that you should not trade everything including your capital, defend your initial capital and aim at making profits. When you make a target and do not meet it, then at least you tried, but trading profusely just to meet the target with limited time is not good at all as it is an offensive approach. You should always protect your capital as it is the only thing keeping you in the business and one mistake can send you to factory reset, i.e; going back to the drawing board wondering when the rain started beating you.

5 Have A Trading Plan

Just like any other venture, Forex trading needs a business plan that has been tested to be working and giving impressive results. The plan involves things that you need to do from A-Z, this may include the rules of engagement, trading pattern, market analysis, and other key aspects that make the business run well. After making the trading plan, you can test it virtually to see if it will go well with the market and if it is good, then give it a green light and start the forex trading. But make sure that you outline the plan as it is the backbone of the whole venture.

6 Know That Trading Is A Business

Forex trading is like a business and should be treated as such for one to get the best out of it by giving the attention it deserves. Other researches have talked about not comparing trading with job opportunities or hobby to be done on leisure time. This means that one should not expect a salary and works on getting profits and give attention and not only focusing on it when you are free. With this, a forex trader will learn to prioritize forex trading just like any other business.

7 Outline Risk

Make sure that you point out the risk you intend to get yourself into and do not give it too much until you are out of business. Do not risk an amount that you cannot afford, risking is only for the amount you are capable of and not anywhere near initial capital. Remember as said earlier, if you lose capital that means that you are out of business and you will not want that to happen to you. Only risk an amount that you know if they go then you will not struggle with bringing back the business into living.

8 Use Technology

The modern era of inventions and innovations can be a plus in forex trading as it helps improve the outcome of a venture. Technology has played a big role in forex trading, thanks to innovators who come with new things every day to enhance the world in bringing people closer. With technology, one can trade anywhere in the world monitor charts using a computer or even mobile phones. This means that one can travel all over the world as well as working at the same time. This has been evident for bloggers and travel entrepreneurs who blog for a living and promote products online while they travel. This can be the same for forex traders and it helps in even having a good time and relaxing the mind while working.

9 Have A Stop Loss

This is somehow similar to outlining risk but specifies the amount that one should be willing to lose in particular trading. In Forex trading, you should only lose what you afford and it is very important to outline the amount or percentage that one should only lose in trading. This also acts as a disciplined mode as it helps in controlling the mind and emotions not to surpass the limited amount of possible risk.

10 Focus On The Bigger Picture

What is the purpose of starting forex trading? Can you make the business to be aligned in that direction? Are you getting some profits and losing sometimes? then you are on the right track heading to greatness in forex trading. Business is not about just making profits but making impacts on a personal level and getting more skills. So what is your bigger picture? To have gained at least 10 per cent in the financial year 2020-2021? Having this in mind, then you can be sure of aiming in the right way as compared to only focusing on maximizing profits.

11 Keep Learning Markets

Forex trading is an ongoing process even after mastering markets and getting out of an amateur venture. One does not stop learning at anything and things keep changing in the forex world this is important to keep an open mind in everything to do with business. Some of the skilled forex traders can fall prey of crowd psychology and some markets are unpredictable making forex trading a learning experience every time one is trading.

12 Be A Progressive Trader

Every forex trader wants to earn profit as it is the main reason for venturing in forex trading in the first place, but are you only profit-oriented the first day in the market or you are moving forward? Learning also can be a huge progress as it helps one avoid making similar mistakes and open ways for more profit in the future. A progressive trade is the one that celebrates every win either small or big as long as it is a victory. Just like a child, you learn to sit then start crawling and in no time you start taking a few steps and eventually running. The same applies to forex trading, you gradually move from one stage to the other and you cannot jump directly to only making profits. You either win or learn. After making a trading plan and testing it, one can join the trading business and encounter ups and downs as it shapes the ultimate goal of forex trading. With this progress, one can be sure of securing a future in forex trading full of experiences and lots of encounters that can prepare you to any hard hurdles that one might come across during your trading experience.

So are you setting up your mind on winning and achieving your goals? If so I suggest you follow the suggestions outlined above and start winning small until you fully master the art of forex trading and rejoice looking at your bank account after meeting your ultimate goals. Remember, forex trading is not a walk in the park and you have to make the right choices.

Conclusion

Many people are turning to trade in order to generate their income, invest in their future, or simply give themselves extra cash for the month. Whatever your reason is for getting into trading, you learned four different types of trading strategies within the contents of this book. First, you learned positions trading, which allows you to hold your position for months to a year. Second, you learned about swing trading, which focuses on the position you hold for a few days to a couple of weeks. Third, you were given some information on day trading, which focuses on buying and selling all your trades in one day and finally learned about scalping trading, which is often called the minute strategy as you hold a position only for a few seconds to a minute or two.

Now you not only understand these four strategies better, but you also understand the basics of forex trading. You also understand the basic risks involved, have the know-how needed to achieve the winning mindset, know how to search for a trusted broker, and how to get a start and gain a profit.

To become a successful trader, you need to continue your education, studying in more detail the type of strategy you want to focus on. This means you have to read more books, research online, join at least one online community and begin talking to a mentor or to more experienced traders who are willing to help and guide you. Even though the market is competitive, people still want to help one another and make sure they have the best possible experience.

Above all, some of the most important steps to remember are the following: do your research, set your daily schedule, have patience, have the right mindset, and be self-disciplined. Also make sure you are paying attention to what the charts show you. You will want to note the candlestick charts, so you can understand if the price in moving in an upward or downward trend. You will also want to look at the trend charts, which will give you a variety of colored lines to explain how well the currencies are performing and if they would be a good fit for you. Taking into consideration all these different factors, you will become a successful trader no matter what strategy you decide to use. One of the biggest parts of becoming successful is believing you can be successful. By following the tips and tricks outlined in this book, you will be able to reach the goal you have set or are about to set for yourself.

Through all the information you have read in this book, you will be able to apply your favorite forex trading strategy. Through practice, you will be able to master your preferred strategy which will allow you to gain bigger profits. It doesn't matter which strategy you decide to use. What matters is that you are confident in your abilities and remain consistent with your strategy.

There are many websites online that offer you the possibility to try out forex trading by using the trading platform in DEMO mode BEFORE you even start trading with real money, and such websites will have to become an integral part of your study as you explore this field of trade.

Remember, good discipline, and good money management are key to being a good trader. Also, not allowing your emotions to run away with you when it is time to make a trade, or when you have heard some news is also imperative. Try as hard as possible to be logical and thorough when it comes to your trading practices, and with time you could be making a 6 figure salary from the comfort of your home.

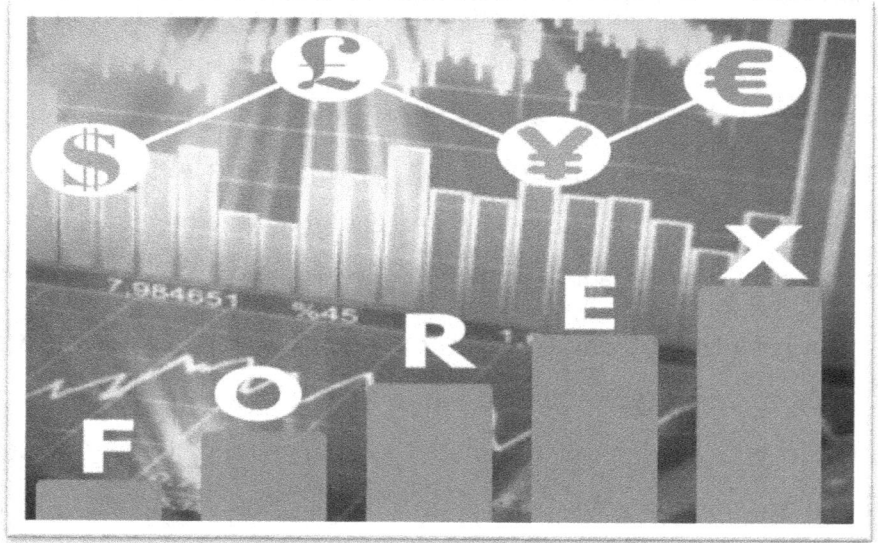

www.ingramcontent.com/pod-product-compliance
Lightning Source LLC
LaVergne TN
LVHW020425070526
838199LV00003B/274